# STRANGE BUT TRUE
# STORIES FROM JAPAN

# STRANGE BUT TRUE
# STORIES FROM JAPAN

by Jack Seward

TUTTLE PUBLISHING
BOSTON • RUTLAND, VERMONT • TOKYO

First published in 1999 by Tuttle Publishing, an imprint of Periplus Editions (HK) Ltd, with editori
offices at 153 Milk Street, Boston, Massachusetts 02109.

ISBN: 0-8048-2130-5

Distributed by

USA
Tuttle Publishing
Distribution Center
Airport Industrial Park
364 Innovation Drive
North Clarendon, VT 05759-9436
Tel: (802) 773-8930
Tel: (800) 526-2778

CANADA
Raincoast Books
8680 Cambie Street
Vancouver, British Columbia
V6P 6M9
Tel: (604) 323-7100
Fax: (604) 323-2600

JAPAN
Tuttle Shuppan
RK Building, 2nd Floor
2-13-10 Shimo-Meguro, Meguro-Ku
Tokyo 153 0064
Tel: (03) 5437-0171
Fax: (03) 5437-0755

SOUTHEAST ASIA
Berkeley Books Pte Ltd
5 Little Road #08-01
Singapore 536983
Tel: (65) 280-1330
Fax: (65) 280-6290

First edition
06 05 04 03 02 01 00     10 9 8 7 6 5 4 3 2 1

Design by Stephanie Doyle

Printed in the United States of America

## ACKNOWLEDGMENTS

I want thank the following persons and organizations for their assistance in research and providing the photographs and illustrations herein:

Kazutsugu Araki, Peter Berton, Faubion Bowers, Rachel Britt, Jo-Ann Cody, Glenn Davis, Ken Edge, Education Committee of Minami Arima in Kyushu, Harry Fukuhara, Tom Fujimoto, Hoover Institution, John Hyde, Sue Lindy, Teruo Masaki of the Tourism Section of the City of Kamakura, Yoshikazu Matsuda, Toshiku Matsumura of *The East*, Amy Meeker, Keizo Mitsuma; Chikyo Oishi of the Bukko-in (Temple) in Kyoto, Mitsuko Sankey, Mihir Sapru, Jim Shaw, *Shukan Shincho*, Vaughan Simmons, John Stephan, Toshiaki Tokai (Director of the Nagasaki Prefectural Library), E. Shane Weaver, and Alvin Yudkoff.

Again, my thanks.

## TABLE OF CONTENTS

*This book is fondly dedicated to my uncle,*
*J.W. ("Ike") Denny of Greenville, Texas.*

# INTRODUCTION

This collection of stories describes real events and people that I learned of or witnessed while in Japan.

There is no link connecting these stories, and each stands alone. All are factual, as much as I have been able to determine. References at the end of each story should help support their reality, as will accompanying photographs.

Some stories are quite well known; others less so. A few I wrote about in earlier works. I hope readers find them as fascinating as I did.

I have given Japanese names in the American style, family names last. Japanese words not likely to be familiar to non-Japanese are in italics. Frequently used Japanese words are not italicized. Although the difference between the long and short vowels in Japanese words and names is vital to aural comprehension, I decided not to use that long mark (the macron) because of typesetting problems.

Jack Seward

# CHAPTER ONE

# Lionhearted Women

*In the West we have too often tended to the extreme view
of the Japanese female: a piteous creature completely sub-
servient to the male of the species, who has no rights, only
duties, and whose life is dominated by three masters: her
father, her husband, and (in her old age) her eldest son.
However, there have been exceptions—and some startling
ones.*

In 1945 Americans arriving in Japan learned that a Japanese woman
walked three paces behind her husband when outside the home, and
that a husband could divorce his wife simply by submitting a written statement of divorce consisting of only 3 1/2 lines (called a
*mikudari-han*).

Her position seemed analogous to that of the Indian woman in the
old following anecdote:

One hot summer day a white man came upon an Indian brave of the
Cheyenne tribe riding comfortably along on his horse with his attractive wife stumbling behind in the dust.

"Why isn't your wife riding, Chief?" asked the shocked white man.

The brave's reply was eloquently to the point: "She no got horse."

The Japanese woman's chief aim in life was to bring comfort and
happiness to her husband, to his parents, and to her children. She was

the first to rise in the morning and the last to climb wearily between the *futon* at night. She stood at the end of the line for the tastier dinner dishes. And in mixed company she spoke only when spoken to.

"If you fall in love with your wife," Japanese men were cautioned "you will spoil your mother's servant."

ONCE IN TOKYO I relayed a dinner invitation from a visiting American to a mutual Japanese acquaintance.

"Mr. (Smith) would like to invite you and your wife out to dinner tomorrow night."

"I would be delighted to accept," said the Japanese man, who I knew to be exceedingly fond of the woman we might have called his better half. "But why my wife? Why on earth should he want to invite her to come along?"

Well, all that has changed, they tell us, at least for the most part. As the Japanese are forever saying—after the war, two things became stronger: women and their stockings.

But by no means were all Japanese women mere "child-bearing house-cleaners" who turned the other cheek and suffered in silence.

In the fourth century AD, for example, the Empress Jingo led an army in a successful foreign conquest (of part of Korea), a feat that no Japanese man was to match for 1,600 years. In ancient Chinese records we find the comment: "The Japanese formerly had kings but after years of civil war, they agreed to crown a woman named Himeko as their sovereign. When Queen Himeko died, a great mound was raised over her and more than a thousand attendants followed her in *junshi* (sacrificial death). After that, a king ascended the throne, but the people would not obey a man, and civil war broke out again. A girl of thirteen named Iyo was then made Queen and civil order was restored."

In the late twelfth century, there arose the Lady Masako Hojo, surely one of the most competent and strong-minded women of any age or country. On the night of her wedding to a Taira governor, she eloped with the renowned warrior Yoritomo Minamoto and ruled Japan at his side until his death in 1199. Thereafter, as the omnipotent Ama Shogun

(Nun General), she continued to wisely control national affairs until her own demise in 1225.

And while not of such historical prominence, there have been more than a few other women who were remarkably lionhearted and steadfast in their policies, affections, and beliefs.

BY WESTERN CALCULATION, O-Shichi was only fifteen years old when the combination shop and residence of her father, a vegetable dealer in Komagome on Tokyo's northeast side, burned to the ground. Until he could rebuild, her father was forced to lodge his family with relatives, and the somewhat plump O-Shichi was sent to stay in the Enrai Temple in nearby Koishikawa (with a priest who was related to her family).

While in the temple, O-Shichi, whose name was written Honorable Seven, met and conceived a grand passion for a fifteen-year-old boy, Sahei Yamada, a samurai's son who roomed in the temple because he and his stepmother were always at each other's throats.

Sahei and O-Shichi felt an exhilarating attraction for each other, and their romance progressed famously until that black day when O-Shichi's father moved into his new shop-house and summoned his daughter to rejoin her family.

Because Sahei's father was a samurai and O-Shichi's was a mere vegetable monger, the couple entertained almost no hope that their dreamed of union would ever receive parental approval. O-Shichi pined away in her loneliness until the night of December 28, in the year of 1682, when a perfectly splendid idea burst upon her—like unto a revelation from on high.

If the fire in her father's shop had been the original cause of O-Shichi's being sent to the Enrai Temple and meeting Sahei, why wouldn't the same cause bring about the same effect again? Good thinking, that.

A girl of great determination, the well-rounded O-Shichi wasted no time touching a torch to the new shop. With this act she preceded Mrs. O'Leary's cow in Chicago by some two-hundred years.

However, the fire spread and burned half of Edo (the early name for Tokyo) to ashes, one of the most devastating conflagrations in Japanese history.

O-Shichi was apprehended and prosecuted, but the kindly magistrate took pity on her youth. He offered her a way out. All she had to do was to affirm in court that she was only fifteen; the magistrate could then give her the much less severe punishment meted out in such cases to persons that age or younger.

However, there was a catch. According to the Japanese way of counting age, O-Shichi was seventeen. She was one year old the day she was born and turned two on the following New Year's Day, even though New Year's Day may have come only a week later.

The local ward master also tried to come to O-Shichi's rescue by declaring (falsely) before the magistrate that his records showed her to be a minor (fifteen or under). But poor, honest O-Shichi did not catch on to the ruse. She steadfastly stuck to the truth, leaving the magistrate no choice.

His sentence on O-Shichi was appropriate, if harsh. After being paraded on a horse through the narrow streets of Edo for hours, she was taken to the public execution grounds in Suzugamori, where, for the crime of destroying half the city by fire, she was burned to death at the stake.

OSAKA, 1587-1600: Lady Komano was the daughter of the general who assassinated former Nobunaga Oda, the dictator of Japan. (The assassin was assassinated soon after that.) Tama (Lady Komano's original first name) had been married at fifteen to the powerful Lord Tadaoki Hosokawa. But after Oda's murder, he divorced her, not wanting to be known as the husband of the woman whose father had committed regicide.

The sedate Tama (Lady Komano) entered no protest but silently obeyed Hosokawa and retired to the mountains of Tamba, where she lived quietly for ten years. Friends advised her to commit suicide, but

Tama replied she could not even do that without a direct command from her ex-husband.

At last Hideyoshi (Oda's successor as supreme ruler) learned of her extreme devotion and chastity and ordered Lord Tadaoki Hosokawa to remarry Tama and restore her to his side as a proper wife.

It was after this that Tama, in need of some kind of spiritual restitution, learned of Christianity and became a convert through the persuasion of her tea master. So devout a Christian did she prove to be that she assiduously studied Latin and Portuguese in order to read the Scriptures and other religious works.

In the turbulent times of May 1600, her husband was sent by Ieyasu Tokugawa (Hideyoshi's replacement) to command an expedition to quell an uprising in the Aizu province. However, Lord Tadaoki learned that a rival of Ieyasu's by the name of Mitsunari Ishida planned to take Tadaoki's wife, Tama, as a hostage. Tadaoki suspected this wicked lord might very well employ some stratagem to entice her into his toils. Before departure, Tadaoki warned Tama that under no circumstances should she be deceived or tricked into leaving the safety of their castle.

But as Tadaoki had feared, Mitsunari Ishida sent an invitation to Tama—who now went by the Christian name Gracia—to pay a visit to Mitsunari's castle. She replied that she could not do so without the permission of her absent husband. Mitsunari then sent a series of similar invitations, each more strongly worded than the previous ones. Finally Mitsunari bluntly wrote that he would send armed men to apprehend her and bring her to him.

Gracia (Tama) instructed her chief chamberlain, Shosai, to reject Ishida's threatening invitations no matter what and to prepare the castle for all eventualities.

There are several accounts of what happened next, but perhaps the most authoritative is one written by a contemporary, a Jesuit priest named Valentine Carvalho, who had heard the story from eyewitnesses:

> *(Gracia) bade all servants and ladies who were with her*
> *to save themselves since only she needed to die, as her*
> *husband had ordered. When they had gone, she knelt*
> *down, invoked the names of Jesus and Mary and bared*
> *her neck with her own hands. Her head was cut off with*
> *a single stroke by Shosai (the chief chamberlain), who*
> *then covered her body with silk clothes, strewed gun-*
> *powder over it, and set it afire.*

Chief Chamberlain Shosai himself committed *seppuku* on the veran-
dah of castle, and all but one of Gracia's ladies-in-waiting managed to
bring their own lives to an end. The one surviving lady escaped from
the castle to carry an account of the death of her faithful-unto-death
mistress to Lord Tadaoki Hosokawa.

Gracia's heroic death seemed to have had a rectifying effect on the
villain of the piece, Ishida, for he repented and released all the hostages
held in his castle. And many of the other *daimyo* (lords) felt a general
sense of obligation to Hosokawa for the sacrifice made by this paragon
of feminine fortitude.

Ironically, Gracia's son, Tadatoshi became a leading general in the
suppression and slaughter of the Christians at Shimabara. (See Chapter
12 about Shiro Amakusa, the Japanese Messiah.)

AT ONE TIME in my chaotic past in Japan, I had a saloon crony named
Ikeda, with whom I shared many a laugh (and cup) in Tokyo's bistros.
It so happened that one of Ikeda's two mistresses was a spry girl named
Hisako, who earned her living as a circus acrobat. When the circus was
in town, it was Ikeda-san's wont to spend two nights of the week in
Hisako's Tokyo quarters locked in God only knows what kind of con-
tortionistic embraces.

Mrs. Ikeda (God rest her) knew nothing about Ikeda's mistress,
Hisako, or for that matter his other paramour, swallowing whole her
husband's adroit fabrications of all-night mah-jongg games and similar
malarkey.

When Ikeda and I got together one Saturday night for a session of *hashigo-zake* (bar-hopping) on the Ginza, he chanced to mention that Hisako was in a state of near-hysteria because he had not visited her at all that week. She had been bombarding his office with frequent phone calls and shrill supplications.

Lady Gracia Hosokawa prepares to be beheaded.
*Drawing by E. Shane Weaver*

The next day, a warm Sunday, I went for a walk. I left my home in Omori, a southern suburb, which was within six or seven blocks of Ikeda's place, and decided to drop by to say hello to my friend and his wife.

Relatives of theirs from the country were there, so I started not to enter, but Ikeda insisted I at least stay for one cup of tea. After I had been introduced, we all sat in the Ikeda's Western-style living room and talked until we heard a knock at the front door. Ikeda left the room to see who it was, and in a moment we heard the sounds of a scuffle.

Just as I was standing up to see if I could be of any assistance—or perhaps to make a run for it—the living room door burst open and in flew Ikeda's mistress Hisako. Wild-eyed and fuming and bubbling at the mouth, she looked around at all of us. Then, without so much as a by-your-leave, she threw herself down on her back in the center of the room. There was a look of grim determination in the set of her mouth, and Ikeda's relatives eyed her in much the same manner that one would regard a rudely awakened wolverine.

"*Hisako desu* (It's Hisako)," Ikeda said weakly to no one in particular, a sickly grin on his face.

"I'm not going to move an inch until you say you will come home with me," Hisako announced in a flat, positive tone while staring fixedly at the ceiling.

At that moment, Mrs. Ikeda entered from the kitchen to find all of us frozen into our individual poses like figures in Madame Tussaud's wax museum. She had been busy preparing a tray of tea and bean-paste pastries for us and knew nothing of the arrival of the latest guest. Although the gracious Mrs. Ikeda had no idea who Hisako was, she rose magnificently to the occasion, and I shall never forget her sangfroid and rectitude.

With all the composure of a great lady, she served the men first, as was only proper, then knelt on the floor beside Hisako. Bowing, she said "*Irasshaimase* (Welcome)." Placing a cup of tea and a small pastry beside this unknown supine guest, she invited her to partake of them. Then, after serving the other women, Mrs. Ikeda retired gracefully and silently to her kitchen.

I muttered something about it being late and started to put on my coat. Ikeda's relatives took my cue and said they would have to hurry to get home before the creek rose. We all departed together, leaving the resolute Hisako still lying there flat on her back, staring stubbornly at the ceiling, and Ikeda looking forlorn and distressed in a chair in the corner. (He told me the next day that he had, in fact, accompanied Hisako to her apartment soon after we guests left.)

I do not know whether Mrs. Ikeda or the nimble and resolute Hisako is more deserving of the sobriquet "lionhearted." Perhaps the term fits them both.

### References

1.  Laures, Johannes. *Two Japanese Christian Heroes*. Tokyo: Charles E. Tuttle, 1959.

2.  Yamaguchi, H.S.K. *We Japanese*. Yokohama: Yamagata Press, 1949.

3.  Feifer, George. *Tennozan: The Battle of Okinawa and the Dropping of the Atom Bomb*. New York: Ticknor & Fields, 1992.

4.  Nishida, Kazuo. "She Chose Death to Dishonor." *Asia Scene*, March 1965.

5.  *Kodansha Encyclopedia of Japan*. Tokyo: Kodansha International, 1983.

## CHAPTER TWO

# Americans Serving Time in Japanese Prisons

*How do Americans fare in Japanese jails? Are they immured in dark, airless dungeons with bread crusts and water-thin gruel once a day and suffering draconian punishments for trifling offenses? Being in a Japanese prison is definitely "hard time," but some Americans prefer it to what they would have received at home.*

### FUCHU PRISON 1979

An American GI, Ed Arnett, was stationed on Okinawa at the time of his arrest by Japanese police for possession of four-and-a-half pounds of marijuana.

During his month-long confinement prior to trial, Arnett was subjected to unrelenting interrogation after which he signed a confession written in Japanese, which he was unable to read. Arnett did not have a lawyer until his no-jury trial actually began. The trial took all of thirty minutes.

With such an inauspicious beginning, you might wonder how Arnett was treated in Fuchu Prison (exclusively for hardened criminals) and what he thought of the prison conditions.

His initial reaction after release was, "I didn't know I could still cry until I went to Fuchu."

Arnett was assigned a nine-by-five-foot cell with a hard, narrow bed and a toilet he could not flush without a guard's permission. He could not write letters, and his incoming mail was censored and limited to one letter a month from his parents. Any packages sent from home were held for him until he regained his freedom.

His meals consisted mostly of seaweed, rice, fish and *miso* soup but no saltpeter, despite the sempiternal suspicion. He lost some sixty pounds during the eighteen months he was incarcerated. Arnett spent fourteen of those months in solitary—a television camera recording his every movement. He could not look out a window nor was he allowed to talk to other inmates. His head was shaved twice a month. He was punished if he touched his bed during the day, or if he was not in that bed after lights-out. He had to work eight hours every day, making paper sacks in his cell. He went to bed at six-thirty in the evening and was roused at the same time the next morning. If he had been well-behaved, he was allowed to see one movie a month.

When asked, Ed Arnett, whose home is in Omaha, Nebraska, states—oddly and astonishingly, it would seem to many—that he prefers the Japanese system of justice to ours. (He has also done hard time in an American prison, so one can assume he has some comparison on which to base his judgment.)

Why?

"Because," Ed replies, "it's fair. The Japanese never tried to trick me. They were always trustworthy—and lenient. I could have received a sentence of five years, but the Japanese gave me only two. The guards at Fuchu Prison were hard, but they never messed with you without good reason ... I'd rather live under a system that's fair than one where the rich guys get off easy.

"American jails are filled with hate," Arnett continues "If the walls of one of our prisons fell down right now, the inmates would all run off—maybe after first killing some guards and visitors. In Japan maybe they would just stroll back to their homes, if they lived nearby."

Or maybe they would remain in their cells, even with the cell doors open. The Kanto earthquake of 1923 actually did fragment the walls of one Japanese penitentiary. Not one prisoner fled, although it would have been simple enough to do so.

Although strict in the extreme, Japanese prisons are exemplary in a number of ways. Most guards go unarmed. In one period of thirty years, there was only a single event that might come close to being classed as a riot. No guard has ever been killed by an inmate, and only one prisoner killed another in a recent stretch of ten statistical years. In the same ten years only forty-one prisoners escaped, while in the U.S. we tolerate more than 8,000 prison breaks every year. There have been no gang wars among the Japanese prisoners and no reported instances of homosexual rape.

In Japan, most criminal cases are tried before three judges who, sitting together, decide the question of innocence or guilt; this system seems to work well. (Chief Justice of the United States Supreme Court, Warren Earl Burger questioned the principle of trial by jury and was quoted in *Time*, June 20, 1969, as saying, "If we could eliminate the jury, we would save a lot of time. You can try a case without a jury in one day that would take you a week or two weeks with a jury.")

In general, the Japanese public does not believe that the ordinary citizen–candidate for jury duty is anywhere near as smart as a judge, which is just as likely to hold true in the United States.

Japan did experiment with trial by jury fifteen years between 1928 and 1943. The accused were given the right to choose between jury trial and trial by judges. The number who chose the former averaged only thirty a year during that fifteen-year period, almost all the accused preferring not to be judged by their peers, so jury trials were abandoned.

The absence of trial by jury is one of the weightiest reasons many Americans watched uneasily when in October 1953, the U.S. Armed Forces gave Japanese courts primary jurisdiction over our military men and their dependents for offenses committed off-base in Japan. They were worried that the Japanese, perhaps still smarting from their defeat in the war, might take advantage of their new authority to punish American offenders more severely than their offenses warranted.

They need not have been concerned. Japanese courts bent over backwards to show leniency to Americans hauled before them. In numerous instances they were so forgiving that they let culprits go scot-free who deserved at least some punishment. Our military prosecutors were forced to seek out other charges (to avoid double jeopardy) with which to bring these presumed evildoers to even lesser justice.

By May 1957, three and a half years later, when the bulk of U.S. forces had left Japan, the Japanese police had apprehended 27,000 U.S. citizens, of whom they indicted only 500 (an arrest-indictment ratio much lower than that for their own countrymen). Approximately half the 27,000 were for traffic violations, of whom only eleven were prosecuted.

Of the five-hundred indicted, about thirty percent were punished by fines alone—and small ones at that. At the end of this period, i.e., May 1957, only thirty-seven American citizens were serving sentences in Japanese prison, none of which exceeded fifteen years. The death sentence was never given to an American, although more than a few Americans had killed Japanese under a variety of circumstances.

The U.S. Defense Department confirmed in a Senate hearing that American offenders generally got lighter sentences from Japanese courts than they would have received from our own (if that can be imagined) and went on to testify that the Japanese had built a special jail for the confinement of American malefactors that was "far and above" the standard for Japanese oubliettes.

TOKYO 1946: A classmate of mine from the Japanese language school at the University of Michigan underwent an experience in a lockup in Tokyo that should be recorded if only to depict the confusion that can arise from cases where the lines of Japanese and American jurisdiction cross and tangle.

This incident occurred in Tokyo shortly after the close of the war in the Pacific. My classmate—we'll call him Pete—was stationed there as a lieutenant and had enjoyed several casual dates with a handsome half-French, half-Japanese girl who worked as a secretary in the office of a prominent American publisher.

Unfortunately, Pete caught the black-market fever that was going around those days and persuaded a Quartermaster Corps truck driver to join him in an effort to make off with a truckload of cigarettes. (A carton of American cigarettes cost sixty cents in the P.X. and brought the equivalent of twenty dollars on the black market.)

The pair was caught; the truck driver was sent to the enlisted men's stockade, while Pete should have gone to the jail for officers. The officers' slammer, however, was filled to capacity, so the Tokyo Provost Marshal decided, just this once, to borrow a cell from the Japanese prison in Sugamo, in Tokyo. So far, so good.

While Pete, the only American inmate, was languishing in Sugamo Prison, he sent a message to the half-French, half-Japanese girlfriend—let's call her Marie—and asked her to visit him. When she came, he somehow managed to convince her that he was innocent of the charge against him, that it was all a ghastly mistake.

Just at that time, a delegation of New York law-enforcement and penology experts came to Japan at Douglas MacArthur's request to survey Japanese prisons and to make recommendations about how to lower the crime rate. (Imagine that: New Yorkers advising the Japanese how to bring malefactors to justice.) This group was headed by Commissioner Valentine of the New York Police Department. Several of these experts had brought their American secretaries with them. One assistant declined the travel opportunity for fear of the dangers lurking on Tokyo streets at night.

Sugamo Prison was one of the first detention houses to be inspected. The prison officials notified all the inmates, including Pete, of the impending visit, instructing them to have their cells spotlessly clean and to be on their Sunday-best behavior.

The main part of the prison was like many in the U.S., six or seven tiers or stories of cells around an open space in the center, laid out so most of the prisoners could see at least part of the floors above and below them. Pete's cell was on the top floor at the end, next to the door leading out from the tier of cells, with the usual hole in the center of its concrete floor to serve for the inmate as a toilet.

Commissioner Valentine and his cohort of male and female Americans arrived at Sugamo on schedule that morning and commenced their inspection. From his top-floor cell, Pete watched as they entered and made their way around the first floor, stopping now and again to ask questions of the Japanese prisoners.

Both the prison officials and the inmates were in a state of nervous excitement; the officials because they could not guess what changes in their working lives this visit might bring about, and the inmates because they were hoping the American visitors would recommend longed-for improvements in bed and board or perhaps even a general amnesty.

My classmate Pete was nervous, too. He was not, after all, a habitual criminal; he had never even been arrested before. But he knew the military courts were handing out increasingly severe sentences for black-marketing.

He and the other prisoners continued to watch as Valentine and his group made their way slowly from the first to the second floor, from the second to the third floor, and then from the third to the fourth floor, the climb taking at least an hour.

While this was happening, Pete began to feel a powerful urge to evacuate his bowels, which would be the first time in three days. The night before, he had asked the prison doctor for a laxative, attributing the cessation of this particular biological function to his mental unrest and tension since being arrested. When Pete arose that morning, the first dose had still produced no effect, so he had taken two additional doses, suspecting the doctor had failed to take his American size into account. (Pete weighed about two hundred pounds.) Although the matter was currently pressing, he determined to try to stifle the urge until the American inspectors had departed from the prison.

After leaving the fourth floor, Valentine's party seemed to disappear. Pete and the other inmates waited nervously for them to reappear at the entrance to the fifth floor, but they did not show up. Five minutes passed. Ten. Then fifteen.

Americans in Japanese prison in Yokosuka pay respects to a guard.
*Photograph by Eddie Adams*

Finally Pete could stand it no longer. He had to use the toilet, that primordial hole in the middle of his cell floor. Convinced by then that the portly Commissioner Valentine and his fellow New Yorkers had left the jailhouse without coming as high as his floor, Pete dropped his trousers and pressed on with the urgent business at hand.

In the very midst of this function, the door to Pete's floor, next to Pete's cell, opened. Through it strode the mighty Commissioner Valentine and his myrmidons; the male and female Americans accompanying him along with several Japanese prison officials, not to mention the U.S. Army staff officers escorting the whole group. Pete told me later that at least two dozen people constituted the inspection delegation.

Passing through the door, they all stopped in front of Pete's cell, fully expecting to find a Japanese prisoner and preparing to ask him questions. Instead of a Japanese, however, they saw before them an American army officer squatting over a hole in the floor, trousers around his ankles.

Pete told me that halting the work upon which he was then engaged would have been far, far outside the limits of his capabilities. The best he could manage was to smile weakly at Valentine and his group and raise one hand in a half-hearted greeting.

When one of the American women in the visiting party espied Pete, she gasped and turned pale from shock, whereupon Pete—for reasons he could never explain satisfactorily, not even to himself—winked at her. Then the entire party hurried on, casting nervous glances over their shoulders.

Surprisingly, this shattering embarrassment ended in Pete's favor. That same night General MacArthur gave a formal dinner for Valentine and his party at the general's residence in the U.S. Embassy, to which he also invited several prominent non-military Americans working in Tokyo. Among them was Marie's boss, whose wife, indisposed that evening, had prevailed upon her husband's secretary Marie to attend in her stead.

During dinner, one of Valentine's party told the august MacArthur about the odd sight they had seen that day: an American army officer confined in a Japanese prison and acting "strangely."

Knowing full well who the officer in question was, Marie plunged into the conversation. "Oh, General MacArthur. I know all about him! He hasn't done anything wrong at all. He's not well and out there in that awful Japanese prison…"

Overwhelmed with compassion, Marie's voice trailed off.

Without hesitation, MacArthur turned to one of the staff colonels standing at parade-rest behind him and grated in a low voice "Get that officer out of there. At once!"

Less than two hours later, Pete had been removed from Sugamo Prison and was being whisked to his old billet, where he was only to be restricted to quarters. Moreover, the Provost Marshal's office was sorely puzzled by El Supremo's sudden interest in the fate of this young lieutenant.

Fearing their decision to lodge an American officer in a Japanese prison might be brought under scrutiny, with unhappy results for them, they decided to drop all charges against Pete and fly him out of the Pacific Theater as quickly as they could.

I heard this story from Pete's own lips soon after his release, just as he was checking out of his billet (also mine) in Tokyo to leave for the airport. Marie, who later married a different American, was there to say a fond farewell and to accept his warm thanks.

### References

1.  Webb, James. "What We Can Learn From Japanese Prisons." *Parade Magazine*, January 15, 1984.

2.  Seward, Jack. *The Japanese*. Tokyo: Lotus Press, 1980.

## CHAPTER THREE

# Phallic Follies

*They loved as few before them have loved, but the white-hot intensity of their devotion brought death to the man and imprisonment to his nymphomaniac true love. The news of their affair—and its bizarre denouement—helped mitigate the tempest threatening Japan's political stability.*

### TOKYO 1936

If a vote were taken to decide what should be Japan's best known, most passion driven and nightmarish love story, the romance of Sada and Kichizo would probably win hands down.

The news of this couple's wild amour dominated newspaper stories in May 1936. Readers found it passing strange that such a weak vessel as the petite, plain Sada could have strangled a strapping fellow like Kichizo. Why had she mutilated her lover in such a macabre way? And just where was the missing member?

Kichizo Ishida managed an inn of the hot-pillow variety in Tokyo with his legal wife. In May 1936, Miss Sada Abe, thirty-one, found employment as a maid at the inn. (She preferred to think of herself as a freelance hooker, but times were hard and even lawyers were looking for more gainful—and honest—work.)

Within one week Sada, who was not especially attractive but was quite nimble and energetic, had smitten Kichizo. The pair decided they were meant for each other for all eternity, then set out to demonstrate the depth of their intoxication. Mrs. Ishida, however, had sharp eyes. She had trod this path before when the itinerant affections of her lustful husband were seen heading elsewhere. Grabbing a broom, Mrs. Ishida ran the gimlet-eyed Sada out of her domain.

Sada retreated to the Masaki, a house of assignation in Arakawa Ward in Tokyo, where she entrenched herself, recouped, and re-established communication with Kichizo. She implored that he join her and prepare himself for a long siege.

Making the excuse of an urgent business trip, Kichizo left his wife and their hostelry and travelled across Tokyo to the Masaki in Arakawa. He had his work cut out for him there, but settled down to it manfully. For six days and six nights, according to later testimony given by the amazed maids employed at the Masaki, he and Sada locked themselves in a marathon-long embrace, breaking apart only long enough to snatch a short nap or a quick snack. The domestic girls were particularly distressed (some would say envious) because at times the lovers would not stop even when one of them entered the upstairs *tatami* room to bring the couple revitalizing sustenance.

On the eighteenth of May, at about eight in the morning, Sada tripped breezily down the stairs and told the maids at the front desk she was going out for a while. With a guileless smile, she asked that they let Mr. Ishida sleep as late as he liked.

At noon, however, Sada had not returned, so one of the domestics decided to ask Kichizo if she should bring him some lunch. A moment later, she came bounding down the stairs, screaming at the limits of her vocal power. Another maid summoned the police without even waiting for her co-worker to regain a semblance of sanity.

The police who had been working overtime for fear of revolutionary violence in the capital found Kichizo strangled with a woman's sash made of pink crepe but what sent the hysterical maid into orbit was the artwork with which someone, presumably Sada, had decorated his corpse.

On his left thigh, the ardent artist had written four characters in blood that read *Sada Kichi futari*, meaning "Sada and Kichizo, we two." On the left arm she had carved the single character for her name, Sada. Then, from an apparently copious supply of blood, she had traced on the sheet in bold strokes five ideographs stating "Sada and Kichizo, we two alone."

What was the primary source of all the blood? She had amputated his male organ with a butcher knife.

Sada's crime immediately captured the attention of a troubled nation. The story was not entirely unwelcome, for it contributed to easing the oppressive tension hanging over Japan like a miasma during the three months following the assassinations and political turmoil of February 26, 1936. Perversely, the heinous castration of Kichizo Ishida—inspired, as it seemed to be, by intense passion—restored the country to a state of equanimity and tolerable good humor. The newspapers and tea shops, the magazines and bars buzzed with excited talk of little else.

Three days later the ever efficient Japanese police arrested Sada in an inn in Takanawa, located on the road leading south from Tokyo toward Yokohama. The arresting officer, Detective Ando, found Kichizo's underwear and personal effects in one of Sada's bundles but not that one object without which Kichizo could not go to the crematorium oven as a complete corpse. Bluntly, Ando asked her what she had done with it.

Shyly, yet fondly, Sada, who was quite jovial about the whole matter, withdrew it, neatly wrapped in high-quality rice paper, from the bosom of her light green kimono, where she had carried it since its severance. Asked why she had taken it to begin with, she replied simply that it was the one object that held for her the fondest memories of Kichizo. Queried about why she had killed her stalwart lover, Sada answered that she could not abide the thought of any other woman having him. Alive, he would surely stray elsewhere. Dead, he was hers forever.

Nevertheless, one of the interrogating detectives was dubious. How, he wanted to know, had a slight, willowy woman like Sada overpowered a man of Kichizo's formidable physique? Sada happily explained that in their joyful sexual experimentation she and Kichizo had discovered that if she applied pressure to his throat while locked in each other's arms and then suddenly released her grip, the surge of temporarily obstructed blood through his veins inflated his phallic weapon, much to the enhancement of their mutual enjoyment. (At first I was doubtful about this phenomenon until I found corroboration in doctors' accounts of executions by hanging, which reportedly produced such engorgement.)

Miss Sada Abe, mistress extraordinaire.
*Courtesy of Mainichi Newspaper*

During their six days of dalliance, inventive little Sada had done this to Kichizo so often that he was not in the least alarmed when she wrapped her pink sash in lieu of her dainty hands around his neck and began to pull it tighter and tighter.

Imagine his surprise when she neglected to undo it.

Charged with murder and corpse mutilation, Sada was brought to trial. She was seemingly indifferent to those allegations until she learned she was also charged with sexual perversion, which infuriated her.

Murder? Yes, she was guilty of that. Mutilating a corpse? Yes, she had done that, too. But no one was going to call her a pervert and get away with it. So, for the first time, Sada took advantage of her right to have legal counsel, and with her lawyer she began to fight to have this cruel accusation stricken from the bill of charges. At length, the court called in expert psychiatric witnesses who testified, after examination, that Sada was not a *hentai-seiyokusha* (a sex pervert) after all but only an *ijo-seiyokusha* (an oversexed person).

Deeply gratified by this vindication, Sada admitted her guilt to the other charges and was given the extraordinarily mild sentence of only six years in prison.

ONE DAY NOT long after the close of the war in the Pacific, I was walking down the streets of seaside Atami, a popular resort town just south of Tokyo, hand in hand with an attractive Japanese maiden who had agreed to guide and instruct me during my first visit. We had just arrived at Atami station and were strolling through town before retiring for the night. As we passed a certain hot springs inn, my "guide" told me—with an unsettling smile—that Miss Sada Abe worked therein.

I knew the story, of course, but I had no idea that Sada was working right there in Atami. All the grim details came flooding back. Nervously, I looked at Yoko (my guide) again and decided I did not care at all for the way she kept smiling at me. (I have since seen the same frightening look alter the features of other Japanese women when the name of Miss Sada Abe is mentioned.)

Deciding caution should be my watchword for the night, I returned to our room, pretended to telephone a number in Tokyo, then announced that an emergency situation at my military unit required my immediate presence in Tokyo.

Not long after that I heard that Sada had left Atami. (Her presence may have had a similar disquieting effect on other male visitors; Atami, after all, is Japan's capital for "weekend honeymooners.")

Some years ago I read that Miss Abe was working as a waitress in a small bar-and-restaurant in Asakusa in Tokyo, but I believe she no longer now inhabits this vale of tears, so Japanese men can sleep more soundly.

SADA'S STORY INSPIRED many other Japanese women to perform similar acts of revenge on men who were in the process of casting them aside for someone else. (Female liberation activists should take close note of the penalties for corpse mutilation.) During the Occupation, one Japanese girl did something as colorful as Sada, if not so final and barbaric, to her lover, an American army colonel.

Since the American colonel's wife was expected to arrive in Tokyo the next morning, the colonel had gone to have one last session with his Japanese girlfriend. His Japanese sweetie had protested and cried and begged, but he took refuge in whiskey and stubborn silence. It was very late when he finally went to sleep on the *tatami* fully clothed and drunk.

As soon as the colonel began to snore, the girl made ready to wreak her vengeance. But instead of amputating it, as charming Sada had done, she merely painted it with red fingernail polish. (If not a manicure or a pedicure, a phallicure?)

The next morning she deliberately let the colonel sleep until the last possible minute, then awakened him brusquely and told him he had only a short while to reach the airport at Haneda to meet his wife's plane. Still dressed but bleary eyed and only half awake, he splashed water on his face and staggered out of her room.

When he got to Haneda, his wife was eagerly waiting for him. He wasted no time loading her luggage into his car and driving them to the Tokyo hotel where they would stay until permanent quarters could be assigned.

As reported to me a few weeks later, he was seriously hung over that morning and in no mood for romantic dilly-dallying. But he feared that if he didn't pretend to be bursting with sexual desire, his stateside wife would, quite reasonably, want to know into what other vessels of release he had been channeling all that energy.

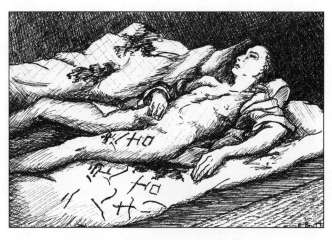

Depiction of Kichizo Ishidaís castrated corpse.
*Drawing by J. R. Britt, Magnolia, Texas*

---

Summoning his wilted forces, he manfully escorted her to the bed in their hotel room and prepared to do the best that he could under the circumstances. But as he disrobed, his wife sighted the splash of color—he later learned that the shade of the fingernail polish was "Flaming Glory"—with which he had been affectionately emblazoned.

Even more astounded than his betrayed wife, he was utterly unable, on the spur of the moment, to think of any explanation at all. Stunned, he could only slump in a chair and stare in disbelief.

The colonel's wife returned to the U.S. on the next available flight. He and his Japanese mistress were soon reunited.

> *Note:* Such perils are by no means limited to Japan. Indeed, one infamous castration recently occurred in the U.S., completely engrossing the nation. And in Thailand, the Southeast Asian paradise, aggrieved wives and true loves habitually sever the offending appendage and either toss it into the yard for the family ducks to squabble over or, in a vivid flight of imagination, tie it to the tail of a kite and watch it soar into the sunset.

### References

1.   *Shukan Shincho*, 1996.

2.   *Mainichi Graph.* 1967.

[See illustration on page 27 to which the following refers]

*One of the many frustrations bedeviling a writer is the acquisition of illustrations with which to color his or her manuscript. A case in point is the above drawing, inspired by a graphic photo of the corpse of Kichizo Ishida, Sada Abe's castrated paramour, just as the Tokyo police found him that fateful day in 1936.*

*I first came upon this photo in the May 30, 1996, issue of a respectable Japanese weekly called* Shukan Shincho, *just after writing the previous chapter with its account of the Abe–Ishida affair.*

*The credit line under the photo read "Courtesy of Koichiro Ichimonbashi"—a name that, incidentally, turned out to be an alias. I wrote to the editor of the weekly magazine, and he forwarded my letter to the Kyoto home of the self-styled "Ichimonbashi," who was then aged and bedridden.*

*Weeks passed. I received no response. At length, I asked my (Japanese) brother-in-law, who had just retired from a career with Mainichi Television, to pursue the matter on my behalf. When my in-law, at last located Ichimonbashi, he—and my request—were coldly rebuffed.*

*I urged my relative not to lose heart but to mail to Ichimonbashi a selection of my books (some in Japanese) and a copy of the award I received from the Emperor of Japan for efforts on behalf of U.S.–Japan friendship. (I am not quite the fly-by-night that Ichimonbashi may have* suspected me to be.) I also authorized my wife's dead sister's husband to offer a considerable sum (well in excess of the market) for one time use of the photo in this book.

By this time Ichimonbashi was in a frothy snit. When my brother-in-law telephoned again, he could hear the old fellow in the background screaming at his wife to tell that "stubborn foreigner" that he would never consent to letting me use the photo of the corpse. His refusal is the main point of this story. He reasoned that "It's all right for Japanese to see that photo, but it would be Nihon no haji (Japan's shame) for foreigners to see it."

And that is why I can offer the reader only this pallid facsimile of the real thing.

—J.S.

## CHAPTER FOUR

# The Mass Hara-kiri at Kamakura

*In 1978, the Reverend Jim Jones led nine-hundred-and-eleven members of his People's Temple Cult in a mass suicide in a South American jungle. But this was not a record. Six and a half centuries earlier, in Kamakura, Japan, an even larger number of the feudal elite eviscerated themselves in order to follow their lord and master in death.*

### KAMAKURA 1333

In the gloom of the thirty-two mat room the *de facto* ruler of Japan, Lord Takatoki Hojo—in despairing dignity—sat cross-legged on a silken zabuton surrounded by bowing courtiers and stern-visaged guards. The flickering torches enhanced the nervous movements of his hands as he filled cup after jigger-sized cup of hot saké for himself. The fact that he did not wait for a servant to pour the rice wine for him was a sure sign of the desperate circumstances.

A frightened messenger crept across the floor of the spacious room and placed himself at the proper distance from the exalted Lord Takatoki Hojo. With his nose still touching the reed tatami, he spoke in the extremely polite Japanese required of the speaker and the occasion.

*"Tonosama, go-hokoku wo mosu node gozaimasu.* (Lord, permit me to submit my report.)"

"*Hayaku mose*! (Speak quickly!)"

"The forces of General Yoshisada Nitta now surround us. Parts of Kamakura are in flames…"

"*Baka*! I can see that for myself. How close is the enemy?"

"Lord, the nearest troops are within two flights of an arrow."

Takatoki dismissed the messenger with a flick of a finger.

"Summon the general of our defending forces!" he shouted.

Takatoki Hojo, ruler of Japan, was thirty years of age on this disastrous night of July 5, 1333. As he always had been, the emperor was secluded in distant Kyoto, living in effete luxury but without significant power. The shogun—the "barbarian-conquering generalissimo"—had long since usurped the reins of hegemony from the emperor's court and had established his own dynasty in Kamakura; here he could keep his lean, Spartan warriors away from the corruptive ease of the emperor's capital, Kyoto.

When Takatoki Hojo was born in 1303, he was destined to govern Japan as regent, the actual power was held by a priest named Enki Nagasaki, his tutor, until Takatoki reached the age of discretion.

It was an incredibly strange situation: a throne, behind a throne, behind a throne, behind a throne. A priest was the true ruler of Japan, but he had to govern through his pupil and ward Takatoki, the regent. To further complicate matters, Takatoki had to issue his edicts in the name of the titular shogun, who was detained in Kamakura, a virtual prisoner. And the shogun had to rule in the name of the living god, the emperor in Kyoto, who was not really a god to anyone.

By the time he reached thirty, Takatoki had wrested control of the regency from the tutor-priest and was finally lord of the Land of the Rising Sun and Ripe Rice-Ears. But all was not well within his realm, not well at all. Disaffected elements throughout the country were demanding a return to Imperial rule; if Takatoki could only hold the Kanto, the immense plain around present-day Tokyo, he might somehow be able to retain his throne—as well as his head.

On 20 June, Yoshisada Nitta, rebellious lord of the Kozuke district in the Kanto, raised his standard in support of the Imperial cause. His several hundred retainers quickly swelled to a prodigious army. What Takatoki most feared—a revolt in his own backyard—had erupted.

A mighty battle was fought on the banks of the Tama River, which flows through Tokyo (formerly called Edo). Takatoki's forces were crushed. By the first of July, they had been driven back to the area immediately surrounding Kamakura, thirty miles south of Edo. The fighting raged with the shrill cries, metal clashing, and multihued pageantry typical of Japanese medieval warfare; but in the rear massive desertions from Takatoki's forces told of an inevitable end to his regency.

The flustered, sweating general summoned by Lord Takatoki knelt and touched his forehead to the matting. His master spoke:

"Tell me frankly—what chance do we have?"

"Lord," replied the general, "with extreme regret, I must tell you that we no longer have a chance of winning. Nor even a chance of holding off the enemy for long."

The dozen long-robed retainers hovering around the youthful Takatoki looked anxiously toward the regent for orders. The eldest and most outspoken bowed deeply, sucked in his breath, and spoke:

"Lord, your life is most precious. We can still flee by sea. Boats will take you to one of the Seven Isles of Izu. We pray you, prepare to escape. Otherwise, that caterpillar Nitta will surely take your life."

IN HIS THIRTY YEARS, Takatoki had never shown much interest in the martial arts. Nor had he ever had an occasion to display bravery in combat or skill in leading his samurai against an enemy. Once out from under the baleful influence of the priest Nagasaki, Takatoki had given himself over to a life of unrestrained revelry to become the outstanding profligate of his day.

Singers and dancing troupes were gathered from all over Japan to entertain the court of the regent, and when their performances were pleasing, they were rewarded with gifts of expensive clothing. Takatoki and his leading courtiers would remove their garments and throw them at the feet of the performers, who later were able to sell them back to court officials for wildly extortionate sums.

Takatoki also developed a mania for dogs and dog fights. His kennels were as large as his entire court and their occupants lived far better lives than the citizens of Kamakura. Dog fights were held on regularly scheduled days of every month; the winners were paraded through the streets, and the common people were required to bow low as the champion dogs passed.

This same Takatoki now displayed an unexpected firmness. After a few minutes of silent contemplation, he spoke in a strong, no longer nervous voice:

"*Kimatta*! (I have made up my mind.)"

Kicking over the tray of saké cups and bottles, he issued rapid-fire orders that sent the courtiers running hither and yon in flurried action, the long sleeves of their robes flowing out behind them making them look like birds in startled flight.

Within an hour, a long, solemn procession, lit by torches in the hands of every fifth man, began to wind its way from the regent's residence near the center of Kamakura in a northeasterly direction, past the Tosho Temple, toward the low hills embracing the town.

The path narrowed as it began its gentle ascent. The rainy season had started, and a steady drizzle was falling. Occasionally, one of the marchers lost his footing on the wet ground and slipped from the path only to clamber back up the slope and re-enter the line.

The grim Takatoki was in the lead. His eldest retainer spoke again from behind him:

"Lord, I beseech you! Do not torment us this way. Let us save you. Even now, the escape boats are waiting."

"None of you has to make this journey with me. I would prefer to go alone."

"No, Lord. Wherever you lead, we will follow."

The retainer fell back to his place in line, sadly shaking his head.

Takatoki soon reached the entrance to a cave that was hardly more than a space scooped out under an overhanging ledge. His attendants quickly spread *tatami* and *zabuton* for him to kneel on. Lord Takatoki now began his final preparations.

About fifty of his retainers—those able to crowd into the constricted space—followed his lead. The rest of the procession knelt in the open space before the cave or took up positions along the path.

It was an eerie scene. A great many warriors and courtiers in full regalia were kneeling in the cave and on the path leading to it. Guttering torches were stuck in the soft ground or tied to tree branches.

"Lord, wait!"

A young girl of striking beauty pushed desperately through the kneeling men up the path, across the clearing, and into the cave. Disregarding court etiquette, she flew to Takatoki's side.

"Let me go with you, please. *Please!*"

The tension left Lord Takatoki's face for a minute. His features softened as he gazed fondly at his favorite mistress, this girl of ineffable loveliness.

She was a renowned beauty from the snow country of northern Japan. Takatoki's wife and son, Tokiyuki, had already been disguised as fisherfolk and been spirited away from Kamakura in a small boat. Takatoki loved his mistress—more than his wife, even more than he loved his dogs, but the Japanese code had demanded he save the life of his wife so she could care for their son and keep the Hojo line from being extinguished on this warm, wet July night in Kamakura.

He nodded his acquiescence to the girl in the colorful kimono and gave a sign—he raised his right forefinger—to the old retainer at his side. The girl sobbed her gratitude. Tears ran down her already rain-wet cheeks.

"Thank you, my lord! Thank you for everything. Now we will never be—"

The old retainer had slipped around behind her and withdrawn his *kozuka*, the small knife attached to the sheath of his long sword. With it, he deftly sliced open her throat's carotid arteries. Warm blood gurgled from her throat and mouth and added yet another color to her kimono as she fell at the side of her master.

Takatoki did not hesitate. Resolutely he thrust his *hara-kiri* knife into the left side of his stomach, just below his waist line. Only a flicker crossed his features. Then he pulled the knife across to the right side. Only the knotting of his jaw muscles showed the excruciating pain he must have felt.

Cave where Takatoki Hojo committed harakiri.
*Courtesy Kamakura City Hall*

At precisely that moment, another retainer, who had been standing ready behind him, lopped off the head of Lord Takatoki with one downward slash of his sword.

An immense sigh—a deep intake and then expelling of collective breath—passed through the assemblage, momentarily drowning out the spattering of the rain and the sputtering of the protesting torches.

That was the signal. The others now began to disembowel themselves. The old retainer who had cut the throat of Takatoki's mistress was among the first to go. Many had asked others to become their *kaishaku* (the *hara-kiri* assistant who cuts off the head after the abdominal cut has been made) and formed couples for a formal minuet.

A few groans, exclamations of surprise, and grated instructions could be heard, but for the most part an eerie silence enveloped the macabre scene. Silence, rain and a deepening darkness.

After the *kaishaku* had performed their grisly duties, they asked others to become *kaishaku* for them— the second round of the ghoulish ball. Eventually, there remained the few who had to die in agony with their heads still attached, without benefit of beheading by an assistant.

A handful of servants had been permitted to accompany the procession. They carried eyewitness reports of the mass *hara-kiri* at Kamakura.

For the wonder-struck General Nitta, the victorious general, they summed up the final moments of the gory scene. More than 870 liegemen had committed *hara-kiri* within a few minutes as had 283 courtiers, Hojo relatives, and assorted retainers. And one girl whose throat had been sliced open at her own tearful request. The total dead exceeded 1,150.

The de-intestined bodies covered the floor of the cave, the clearing in front of it, and as much of the path leading back down to Kamakura as could be seen. More than a thousand headless trunks pulsed forth hundreds of gallons of blood, to drench the already soggy earth.

Many of the heads that had been sliced off had rolled down the adjacent slope, catching on stones and shrubs along the way—only to be dislodged by others following the trails of blood from above.

As the awed servants withdrew, the rain increased in force and the last few torches sputtered out. Besides the rain, the only sounds were from occasional owner-less heads seeking their forlorn way farther and farther down the slope.

In addition to those who died on the hillside, more than six thousand others faithful to the Hojo cause of Lord Takatoki somehow made their exit from this world. More took the tonsure and became religious recluses; others simply disappeared.

### References

1. Papinot, E. *Historical and Geographical Dictionary of Japan*. Tokyo: Charles E. Tuttle Co., 1972.

2. Morris, Ivan. *The Nobility of Failure*. Tokyo: Charles E. Tuttle Co., 1975.

3. Seward, Jack. *The Japanese*. Tokyo: Lotus Press, 1980.

4. *Japan, The Official Guide*. Tokyo: Tourist Industry Bureau, 1963.

5. Sansom, George. *A History of Japan*. Tokyo: Charles E. Tuttle Co., 1974

# CHAPTER FIVE

# A Second Israel?

*It was a shining vision to thousands, maybe even millions, of Europe's Jews, safe from the hazards of ethnic barbarities, working in the burgeoning industries of a raw, new land, free to open their own businesses and practice their religion. The Jews would be far removed from pogroms and warnings of "Juden Raus!" Where could such a promised land be? In Israel? No, it would be many thousands of miles from the lands of the Bible.*

## HARBIN, MANCHURIA 1933

In 1905, by the provisions of the Treaty of Portsmouth, Japan received the immense South Manchurian Railway as a plum for winning the Russo-Japanese War. Promptly, the victor dispatched the Kwantung Army to guard its new railroad.

Even before 1905 Czar Nicholas II of Russia had been encouraging Russian Jews to migrate to Manchuria to enhance his country's influence in the vast underdeveloped lands he had wrested from China not long before. By 1931, some 13,000 Jews had settled in Manchuria, soon to become Manchukuo. In that same year Japan decided to envelop this raw frontier-land in its own sheltering arms, so the Soviet Union would not beat them to it.

A Japanese clique known as the Manchurian Faction, made up of certain bureaucrats and military officers emerged. They held to the belief that expansion onto the Asian continent, including, of course, Manchuria, was a likely road to Japan's national destiny. More precisely, they hoped to "develop sparsely populated Manchuria into a 600,000-square-mile buffer zone" against the feared incursions of the Soviets.

Two leaders of the faction were Colonel Seishiro Itagaki and Lt.-Col. Kanji Ishihara. Another keenly interested observer was Baron Korekiyo Takahashi, the vice-governor of the Bank of Japan. The Baron had persuaded Jacob Schiff, a partner in the New York investment firm of Kuhn-Loeb, to lend Japan five-million-pounds sterling when it was desperately needed to purchase armaments for the Russo-Japanese War.

The plan to populate Manchuria seemed an excellent idea, but the formidable barrier to its attainment was raising the required capital; the Faction calculated that about $100,000,000 would be needed to settle 30,000 Jews on the empty plains to the northeast of China proper. Thus, capital and immigrants (or refugees) were the keys to the Faction's ambitions.

The Japanese people had already showed a marked distaste for emigration of any kind. Even their northern island of Hokkaido was notoriously underpopulated, and they could not be relied upon to send their sons and daughters to populate foreign lands.

The party primarily responsible for the Manchurian development, if indeed it could ever be brought about, was the mastodonic South Manchurian Railway. Yoshisuke Ayukawa, a low-class iron-monger with a repugnant personality, now steps forth onto the stage of this strange play. Ayukawa had studied steel-making in the United States, then returned to Japan to create the titanic industrial combine known as Nissan. The South Manchurian Railway asked entrepreneur Ayukawa to teach them how they should go about developing Manchuria from a wilderness into a broad land of busy factories, bustling urban centers, a solid infrastructure, and banks designed to channel torrents of gold to the mother country.

Ayukawa took counsel with Baron Takahashi, an old crony, and Yosuke Matsuoka, who was president of the railway and soon-to-become Japan's foreign minister. (Matsuoka was the player who angrily led Japan's delegation out of the League of Nations permanently.)

After considerable thought and investigation, the repellent Ayukawa suggested that the railway look to the Jews for a solution to their problem. The Jews, Ayukawa explained, were energetic, business-minded, creative, and often possessed of financial resources, although not as much as he seemed to believe.

The huge railway corporation took the iron-monger's advice and put the Manchurian Faction together with some "Jewish experts" in Japan's armed forces; principally, Captain Koreshige Inuzuka and Colonel Norihiko Yasue, also posing as a Russian-language specialist.

Some years would be required for the plan to culminate but something informally called the Fugu Plan was hammered into shape. As a starter, Ayukawa—to test the waters—published a "Proposal to Invite 50,000 Jewish Refugees to Manchuria." Ayukawa detected no strong opposition to this proposal and was much encouraged.

Captain Inuzuka named the project the "Fugu Plan" after the puffer-fish (also globefish or blowfish) whose raw flesh is ambrosial—at least to Japanese tastes—but must first have the lethal poison (tetrodotoxin) in its liver and ovaries excised by licensed chefs.

Inuzuka was comparing the Jewish refugees and the plenitude of communists among them to the puffer-fish and its mortal tetrodotoxin. If only the Jewish communists could be excluded, the capitalist and socialist Jews remaining would be the delectable flesh of the otherwise deadly fish.

IN EUROPE Adolf Hitler—with his magnetic voice and piercing eyes—became chancellor of Germany on January 30, 1933; three months later he ordered a boycott of Jewish businesses in Germany. More and more German Jews now began to understand the perils that might be awaiting them, and they fled Germany in growing numbers. (In 1937, 23,000 left legally; 33,000 the following year.) Word reached some of their ears of a possible haven called Manchuria. A haven perhaps, but not quite a land of milk and honey.

The Manchurian Faction in Japan wanted the Jews to migrate, but they did not want to appear to be too supplicatory in extending their invitation. Instead, it suited Japan's purposes to have the Jews come to them knuckling their forelocks.

In any event, it would profit Japan to paint Manchuria in glowing colors. After all, there were other benefits of living conditions for Jews in cities Harbin, Darien, and Port Arthur that might not encourage refugees. One of the deterrents in Manchuria was the presence of anti-Semitic Russians who had fled there in the twenties and had become, if not prosperous, at least a stable and not-inconsiderable percentage of the population. These Whites, especially those of a mischievous turn of mind, were not above harassing the Jews. Their favored weapon was to kidnap them and make demands for huge ransoms. This became a common crime.

So, on one hand the Japanese—at least the Manchurian Faction—wanted to encourage Jewish immigration to Manchuria. On the other hand, reports of kidnapping, extortion, and other crimes spoke loud tones of discouragement.

Then, in 1933, an outrage occurred with the potential of doing serious harm to Manchuria's uncertain reputation as a safe haven—the abduction of twenty-four-year-old Simon Gaspe of Harbin, Manchuria.

The year before the tragedy of Simon Gaspe in Harbin, Manchuria, the Charles Lindbergh baby had been stolen from his parents' home in New Jersey, the curtain-opener in what was quickly to become one of the two "circus trials" of the twentieth century. If the murder of Simon Gaspe had been committed elsewhere—in the United States, for instance—it might easily have captured as much media hysteria as the Lindbergh baby or perhaps even O.J. Simpson's *cause célèbre* in Los Angeles. The Gaspe case certainly offered many of the elements that caught the attention of a lachrymose, scandal-starved public in both the Lindbergh and Simpson happenings.

Simon Gaspe was abducted when the Manchurian Faction could not afford the dissemination of any news about Jewish maltreatment in Manchuria.

On the evening of August 24, 1933, young Simon Gaspe (his name is sometimes spelled "Semyon Kaspe") was accompanying Miss L.

Shapiro to her home when two fascistic White Russians hired by Japan's secret police kidnapped and transported him blindfolded to a hideout thirty-five miles west of Harbin. (Thus, one Japanese organization evidently was working against the best interests of another. Such a conflict should not be surprising. For instance, the Japanese army, which looked upon Manchuria as its private preserve, often locked horns with the Imperial navy, which carried more clout in the southern ports along the China coast.)

Simon's father, Joseph, had emigrated from Russia to Harbin in 1907. At first he was a pawnbroker but he soon became a successful gem merchant and used his profits to buy a hotel (the Moderne), a restaurant, and several movie theaters. Along the way, he somehow obtained French citizenship for himself and his family, although he may never had trod French soil.

His son Simon was a concert pianist who had graduated from the famed Conservatoire de Musique in France. He had just made a concert tour of several international cities and planned to spend the summer relaxing in his father's mansion in Harbin.

Events involving the kidnapping moved forward along intricate paths and at a smart clip. The White Russian hoodlums sent the father, Joseph Gaspe, a ransom note demanding $100,000. Joseph counter-offered $12,000. The kidnappers expressed their contempt for this stingy sum by mailing Joseph half of one of Simon's ears.

Joseph still refused to come to terms, either from obsessive parsimony or stubborn unwillingness to truckle to intimidating threats. Instead, he requested the advice and intervention of the French vice-consul, a Monsieur Chambon, in the city of his residence. Even the wily lawyers defending O.J. Simpson might have been appalled had they been confronted the knotty twists that hove into view in the city of Harbin.

While poor Simon's fate still hung in a balance, the evidently competent agents of Vice-Consul Chambon snared the youngest of the abductors, a teenager by the name of Komisarenko, who lost no time in betraying his friends and giving up their names.

While the French diplomat was preparing charges against this entire gang in court, the Japanese secret police, who had inspired the kidnapping to begin with, got their own hands on the perfidious Komisarenko and spirited him to a remote area that happened to be on the right of way of the South Manchurian Railway.

Alarmed, the secret police felt that what control they might have had over these somber events had begun to slip away from them.

Suddenly, a new player emerged from the wing: Colonel Fukashi Oi, head of the vaunted security forces of the South Manchurian Railway. He learned the whereabouts of the teenage White Russian punk Komasarenko and arrested him on property owned by the Railway. This enabled Oi to keep the young Russian in his own custody.

Next, the secret police took all the French Vice-Consul's agents off to their own lock-up, and on November 28, 1933, Colonel Oi's men nabbed two more of the abductors. (It should be mentioned that Colonel Oi was an honorable man of old samurai stock who despised the secret police of his own country.) Colonel Oi's captives revealed the location of Simon Gaspe's torture pit, but the secret police got there first, because they knew all along where it was.

Simon's travail ended there. He was either dead of starvation, mistreatment, and exposure when the secret police lifted the lid of his prison pit—or if there was still a faint vapor of life in his gangrenous, mutilated body, they lost no time snuffing it out.

In Harbin, there was still a native Manchurian structure of police and courts, and it was in one of these courts that the trial of the Gaspe kidnappers began. It lasted two years, until 1936, when the Chinese judges handed down sentences of "death by hanging within three days" to six of the White Russian criminals, while the remainder of the gang was assured they would spend many years in prison.

No more than two days had passed after these sentences were announced than Kwantung Army Chief of Staff General Seishiro Itagaki threw out the verdicts. He arranged for the Chinese judges and the prosecutorial staff to be apprehended on trumped-up allegations. A new trial to be held in Japanese court was ordered. The upshot of this travesty was that the kidnappers were set free and even given employment by the Japanese secret police.

WHEN JOSEPH GASPE was taken to view the corpse of his son, he went mad. Soon thereafter, with his French wife, he disappeared into the oblivion of history.

Молодой талантливый піанист С. Каспе, убитый 24 ноября.

Simon Kaspe, the pianist.
*Courtesy of the Hoover Institution (Rubez, December 9, 1933)*

By now the future did not bode too well for the Jews in Manchuria.

Still, the Manchurian Faction and its military "Jewish experts" persevered. Increasing numbers of Jewish refugees were crowding into European ports, seeking passage to sanctuaries in other countries. The Faction members continued to circulate and often modify their plans for the resettlement of masses of Jews in Manchuria. They spoke of numbers as high as one million. True, they admitted, this and that had unfortunately happened, but nothing had really changed. With support from within Japan and capital from American Jews and the refugees themselves, adequate funds could still be amassed, they promised.

To obtain the financial support of American Jews the planners decided to first secure the backing of Rabbi Stephen S. Wise, president of the almighty American Jewish Congress. Why, they asked rhetorically, would a powerful rabbi refuse to cooperate and send much-needed succor to the multitudes of his fellow Jews suffering in Europe? With much optimism, they dispatched a Mr. Tamura—carrying introductions from several prominent persons—to describe to Rabbi Wise the benefits that could be derived from the Fugu Plan and to request—on bended knee—the rabbi's blessing.

At about this time an organization of Shanghai Jews dispatched its own delegation to entreat the same Rabbi Wise to help *prevent* more Jewish refugees in Europe from setting forth for destinations anywhere in China, where, the Shanghai Jews averred, there already lived too many of them. Continuing and even greater infusions of their fellow ethnics would only render already difficult situations more intolerable.

Rabbi Wise decided to stand aloof from proposals to channel aid from the United States to any group, even one constituted of Jews, based in any territory governed by Japan.

One interpretation—only one, mind you—of Wise's stern rejection of the supplication was that the good rabbi was an American first and a Jew second. His heart might ooze blood for his fellow members of the tribe of Moses, but aid sent from the United States to persons of any race living in a land under the hegemony of Japan (to him, rightly, a potential enemy of the first water) would constitute a traitorous act.

The blows continued to fall on the Japanese dream of glittering Jewish cities on the Manchurian steppes. In 1938, Gisuke Ayukawa concluded that there was no hope of obtaining the needed capital from America. He still supported the Fugu Plan but asked his collaborators to seek funding elsewhere.

In July 1940 Japan signed the Tripartite Pact with Italy and Germany, becoming an official ally of Germany, the *bête noire* of world Jewry.

And, of course, in 1941, the minions of the Imperial Navy's Admiral Isoroku Yamamoto delivered a crippling blow to the U.S. navy peacefully at anchor in Pearl Harbor, Hawaii. The final curtain had fallen on the Fugu Plan.

Kidnappers of Simon Kaspe (Russkie Slovo, December 5, 1933)
*Courtesy of the Hoover Institution (Russkie Slovo, December 5, 1933)*

Even the 13,000 Jews then in Manchuria sought other sanctuaries such as Shanghai. Yet, in later years, a light would gleam in the eyes of the Fugu Plan's adherents. Just think, they would fantasize, what we might have accomplished if fate had only dealt us a few more good cards.

IN KAMAKURA, JAPAN, in the 1960s, I worked on a certain historical research project with Dr. Setsuzo Abraham Kotsuji, the Japanese author of a textbook on Hebrew grammar and a participant in the Fugu Plan events. He had, in fact, been employed by the South Manchurian Railway as its Jewish affairs advisor. He and I spoke several times of the ramifications of that refugee resettlement project.

Even though it was not long before his own demise, Abraham Kotsuji still waxed with youthful eloquence about what might have come to pass. "Just think," he said, "hundreds of thousands of Jews might have been saved. And the possible effects on world events defy the imagination."

Rabbi Stephen Wise of the American Jewish Congress surely acted from patriotic American persuasions in turning not supporting Fugu Plan; but viewed from a historical perspective, one wishes the rabbi had been somewhat more magnanimous toward the refugees who might have settled in Manchuria.

In 1939, when Japan might well have enlarged the projected number of Jewish immigrants to Manchuria to hundreds of thousands, Wise stood solid against any effort at refugee salvation that might also benefit Japan.

A successful Fugu Plan would have showered economic, political, and military awards on Japan, but these successes could well have militated against Japan's risking hostilities in the Pacific. Russia was already warring with Japan along the borders of Outer Mongolia and Manchuria, and a burgeoning industrial structure and population in the latter could have made the Soviets rethink the chancy business of pushing south across the Manchurian border, as they eventually would in August 1945.

Furthermore, Britain and Germany would have been given cause to ponder their own international alignments and aims if they perceived a more prosperous and stronger nation arising in the center of a troubled region in East Asia.

Most importantly though, the Fugu Plan would have saved lives. A great many.

## References

1. Tokayer, Marvin, and Mary Swartz. *The Fugu Plan.* New York: Paddington Press, 1979.

2. Bergamini, David. *Japan's Imperial Conspiracy.* New York: William Morrow, 1971.

3. Yamaguchi Shigeji. *Higeki no Shogun: Ishiwara Kanji* (Tragedy's General: Ishiwara Kanji). Tokyo: Sekai-sha, 1952.

4. Yoshihashi Takehiko. *Conspiracy at Mukden, The Rise of the Japanese Military.* New Haven: Yale University Press, 1963.

5. Krasno, Rena. *Strangers Always: A Jewish Family in Wartime Shanghai.* Berkeley: Pacific View Press, 1992.

## CHAPTER SIX

# An Unusual Character from the Past

*He knew the temples and taverns, the alleyways and beach-front villas of the historic town as well as anyone. Living in a cottage beside the statue of the Great Buddha, he often lingered there to meet American tourists. He was a veteran of the Great War and married to a Japanese woman, who presented him with a son when he was sixty-nine. If you knew him, you would not forget him.*

## KAMAKURA 1964

The elderly, balding white man strolling the streets of the ancient town was a well-known sight to the residents of Kamakura and the circum-ambient area. Still stiffly erect, he walked along at a good clip—but stopped often to pass the time of day with shopkeepers, policemen, and other pedestrians. They all knew him, and many of his stories.

The locals seemed to relish these moments of communication with him, perhaps because this gave them a chance to practice their English or to catch a glimpse of the world outside Japan, through the colorful experiences and bold opinions of this American senior citizen. They regarded him with affection and with some degree, I think, of amazement, for surely he was to them a *hen na gaijin* (strange foreigner). At least, that is how they often described him.

He was over sixty when he first came to Japan. He took to the country and the people quickly and lived there until his death ten years later. He was called "Pop" by many, so I will use that name herein.

Pop found a job on the U.S. Yokosuka Navy Base as a housing engineer and in his charge had approximately one hundred "private rentals" located throughout the Miura Peninsula from Oppama to Kurihama and west as far as Chigasaki. It was his job to find and rent a house, make necessary repairs, furnish it and employ maids, gardeners, and boiler men. When the new American family arrived from the U.S., he would assign them to a house of the proper size in a convenient location, help them move in and get settled, and perform many other services and favors (including sending a bouquet of flowers to the wife in her new home). When the family finally returned to the U.S. two or three years later, he went through the same process, only in reverse.

Understandably, Pop was well known in that part of Japan. His hundreds of acquaintances included house owners, real estate agents, plumbers, carpenters, electricians, municipal officials, gardeners, maids, and, of course, the many Americans whose needs he serviced. It was his habit to report to his Yokosuka office early and get through with his "paper work" by mid-morning, after which he was free to start on his rounds for the day.

Pop tried to visit as many of his houses as he could every day, in order to make safety inspections, supervise requested repairs, mediate lessor–lessee disputes, consider requests for new or different furnishings, solve maid problems, and pay rents. His red jeep station wagon became a familiar sight on those roads.

When the end of the month came around, his arrival was noted with even keener anticipation than usual, inasmuch as he would be carrying millions of yen to pay rents and salaries. He carried these huge sums in a footlocker placed behind the driver's seat in his station wagon. He was never robbed, and he never misplaced a single one yen.

When he wasn't carrying cash in this footlocker, it pleased him to fill it with PX merchandise: candy, chewing gum, hose, cigarettes, coffee, tea, sugar, and other items. It was then the footlocker became what he liked to call his "treasure-chest." He was forever opening it to give a present to a child at the side of a road or to a maid with a sick relative or to an old lady sunning herself beside a temple. He spent half of his salary or more to keep his treasure chest filled.

Pop never took anything in return for these gifts and favors. Friends tried to invite him out in the evening, but it was his firm rule to be in bed by 7:00 (and up the next morning at 3:30). Real estate agents and house owners tried to give him expensive gifts or kick-backs, but these were courteously and firmly refused. Almost anyone who came to him with a hard-luck story was sure to get a gift of $15 or $20 in Japanese currency. So generous was he with his money that those who loved him tried to keep needy people away from him, lest he pauperize himself.

Even before coming to Japan, Pop's career had been unusual. Born in Syracuse, New York, he began delivering milk when he was only eight years old to help support his mother and two sisters. At sixteen he went south to Texas, enlisted in the army and pursued Pancho Villa into Mexico. During the First World War, he was a captain in the field artillery.

After the war, he worked for many long years as an actuary in an insurance company in Tulsa, Oklahoma; but in the midst of the Depression, he decided he wouldn't see much of life or of the world behind a desk, so he quit (which took a lot of courage in those difficult times) and worked for a while as editor of an oil industry magazine, and then as manager of a bakery. In 1938, he became manager of an 11,000-acre cattle-and-wild-animal ranch outside Bartlesville, Oklahoma, where he stayed until the middle of World War II. He became dissatisfied with having no role in the war effort, so he tried to enlist in the Army but was turned down because of his age.

For a while he worked in a defense plant in Tulsa, but that didn't satisfy him either. He found a job as a civilian at an Air Corps base in Alaska (in the hope, I think, that the Japanese would attack there and he could get in on the fighting). After the war, his urge to see more of the world persisted. After a year building houses in Siloam Springs, Arkansas, he worked on an orange-and-walnut ranch in southern California, as a "gandy-dancer" with a railroad construction crew in Wyoming, as a PX manager on Eniwetok and Kwajalein in the Pacific, and as manager of a small hotel on Maui. He first went to Japan after working in Hawaii.

John N. Seward Sr. in World War I.

He was single, long divorced from his first wife. At length, in Kamakura he found a Japanese woman who pleased him. The feeling apparently was mutual, and they were married. Then, at the age of sixty-nine, Pop became a father for the second time. (He had also sired a son by his first wife.)

Happy about this development, Pop lost no opportunity to exhibit his second son, and during the warmer months, he was often seen pushing the baby carriage through the streets of Kamakura. Acquaintances would stop and ask if the baby was his grandchild. In pretended indignation at the affront to his virility, Pop would rear back and make it clear, in stentorian tones, that this was his son, not his grandson.

John N. Seward Sr. with second son.

Having retired from his job on the Yokosuka navy base, Pop settled down with his wife and baby to a comfortable existence in a small house by the Daibutsu in Kamakura. In reasonably good health and still strong for his age, it was his practice to walk five to ten miles daily. He also shopped, read a great deal, visited friends, made useful things with his hands, and traveled around Japan.

He was enjoying his retirement years, but in December 1964, he fell ill with a sickness his Kamakura doctor could not diagnose. Taken to Tokyo by ambulance, he was found to be suffering from gas gangrene, the same germ that killed so many soldiers in World War I.

The only hope of saving his life was use of a high-pressure oxygen chamber, but the only one then in the Far East (other than the one in the

Yokosuka Navy Hospital—which was off-limits even to a World War I veteran) was in the Tokyo University Hospital. He was rushed there, operated on, and placed in the hyperbaric oxygen chamber. His was the first case of gas gangrene the hospital had seen in more than twenty years, so eleven of its staff doctors stood by in curious attendance. Despite their best efforts, they were unable to save Pop and he died two days after Christmas. He was survived by the son of his first marriage, his widow, and his second son (then two years old).

The reader may wonder why I know Pop's story so well. It is because his name was John Neil Seward, my father.

John N. Seward Sr. in World War I

### Reference

1.   *Tokyo Weekender*, February 9, 1990.

John N. Seward Sr. in front of Buddha statue in Kamakura.

# CHAPTER SEVEN

# Three Extraordinary Geisha

*What women these three geisha must have been! One became the mistress of a prime minister. Another was an armless wonderwoman. The third married into the House of (J. Pierpont) Morgan. These practitioners of the arts may be a dying breed, but when they are gone, what strange tales of tragedy and triumph they will have left behind them.*

## OSAKA CIRCA 1907

Tsuma-kichi was her geisha name, and one of her several talents was that she was a superb performer of what the Japanese call posture dancing. She was so good, in fact, that she earned a dancing teacher's certificate while she was only fourteen—the first woman (girl, really) to do so that young.

Not much older, she was sent—a full-fledged geisha—to a bagnio in Osaka's licensed quarters. There, a flesh monger by the name of Manjiro Nakagawa became her "guardian."

Tsuma-kichi was the fifth geisha to enter Manjiro's house. The sixth woman under his roof was his termagant wife, O-Ai, an obscene woman whose drunken escapades and capacity for mischief eventually pushed poor Manjiro to the brink of insanity.

One night O-Ai, who was shunned by the neighbors as a hysteric, went off on another toot and tear. Despairing of ever enjoying a quiet family atmosphere in the bosom of his courtesans, Manjiro, whose face was deeply pockmarked, went out alone to see an inspirational play, *The Murder of Ten*. On his way back home, he dropped in at a dramshop to brood and tank up. Befogged with saké, he determined to set the world to rights. He would do no less than smite the wicked.

When he was finally asked to leave the dramshop, he staggered off to his bagnio, the Mountain Plum Tree, sowing alarm and discord all the way. Getting his heirloom sword out of a closet, he climbed the stairs and slashed to death the four innocent geisha sleeping on the second floor. He next descended the steep stairs and entered the room where he and his ogress of a wife O-Ai slept. In the blackness of the room, he tripped over a futon, waking up O-Ai. Querulously, she came to her senses and started to berate her husband for disturbing her saké-induced rest. Manjiro, sword held behind his back, was in no mood to bandy words with this slattern. Happily, he walked around to her side of the futon and neatly decapitated her.

Only one woman was now left alive in Manjiro's small world, and unfortunately it was our heroine Tsuma-kichi. When she saw the master of the Mountain Plum Tree enter her room with bloody sword in hand, she was paralyzed with fright and prayed he would go away or somehow be distracted, but unfortunately he was not to be denied his alcohol-inspired vengeance on all womankind. He gave Tsuma-kichi three mighty whacks, the first which completely severed one arm, the second which cut off all but two inches of the other arm, and the third which dealt the unfortunate geisha a powerful slash across the face, knocking out most of her teeth. Manjiro then left the bloody charnel house to spend the night comatose in an alley.

The next morning a neighbor, puzzled by the unnatural stillness at the Mountain Plum Tree, went in to investigate. What she found caused her to leave screaming. When the police and a doctor arrived, they were surprised to find Tsuma-kichi still alive, despite the loss of copious quantities of blood. Despairing of her chances, the doctor shook his head at the ambulance attendants who came to carry her away.

However, Tsuma-kichi was blessed with one characteristic she would need later in mammoth quantities—tenacity. Although her not completely severed arm had to be amputated, she clung to life and survived.

After recovering her strength, she enjoyed considerable popularity for a while as the "Armless Geisha," but once the public's curiosity had been satisfied, she taught herself to hold a brush with her teeth and her toes. She became quite adept at calligraphy, painting, and writing poetry.

In the meantime, she had married a painter and borne him two sons, but her husband abandoned her, so she had to rely on her brushwork to support the children and see them through school. In 1956, at the age of 67, she became a Buddhist nun in Kyoto.

(It is interesting to note how many geisha have shaved their heads and become nuns in their declining years; the number is entirely out of proportion with that of the rest of the female population. Gio and Shizuka Gozen—both twelfth-century *shira-byoshi* (progenitors of the geisha)—may have set this fashion. The former fled from the palace of Kiyomori, head of the Taira clan, but was forced to take refuge and spend her remaining years in a nunnery. The latter became well-known as the inseparable companion of Yoshitsune, Japan's famous warrior, and donned the cloth after his death.)

## KYOTO, EARLY 1900s

In Kyoto's geisha district—the Gion—there arose like the morning sun a beautiful geisha of the Japanese style. She was likened to a fabled princess in a fairy tale. Because top-ranking geisha are usually treasured more for their accomplishments than for their physical attractiveness, this new star in Gion's firmament was held more in awe because she had both.

In the beginning of her employment, she called herself Hatsuyuki (First Snow) but not long afterwards she changed her name (at the urging of a fortune-teller) to Oyuki (Honorable Snow). The names geisha give themselves are sometimes poetic, sometimes downright weird.

Many customers tried to win her heart or at least her body. The man who first had carnal knowledge of Oyuki is not recorded, but someone must have, for it was never claimed she was a virgin after achieving full-fledged geisha status.

One account of Oyuki's life tells us that she had a passionate liaison with a college student but his parents forced him into a more conservative union. (Many geisha are said to have had the love affairs of their life with a student. There is no way to prove or disprove the veracity of such suppositions, but the academic world and the demimonde are such discrete spheres in Japan that one wonders just where and how all those poor students got together so often with the usually very expensive geisha.)

With a strong nose and beautiful eyes, Oyuki (Yuki Kato was her birth name) also outshone her colleagues linguistically, for she alone had some smattering of English. Just when Oyuki had ascended the heights of geisha-dom in Japan's cultural capital, who should enter her life but George Denis Morgan, nephew of the affluent John Pierpont Morgan. Pierpont's nephew was circumnavigating the globe and keeping the world's distilleries working nights.

His energies had not flagged in the least when he reached Kyoto in 1905. Setting up his command post in a teahouse called Ichirikijaya, he began to sample the geisha of the Gion district. Having to use an interpreter, however, hampered the progress of his dalliance, so when he heard of one of Gion's heavenly bodies who had a modicum of George's native tongue, he arranged for Oyuki to be next in line.

Several days passed before Oyuki could make room for George in her already full schedule, thereby whetting his appetite and quickening his pulse. And when she did at last appear, the waiting line ended with her. George was thoroughly ensnared and soon proposed marriage. When she accepted, he gladly paid a very large amount of money to buy her out of the bondage of her contract.

Yuki Kato had become Oyuki Morgan, a genuine member in good standing of the opulent Morgan clan. While she had been a star in the sky over Gion, she had enjoyed a comfortable enough life-style, but it had been as nothing compared to what awaited her.

Later in 1905, Mr. and Mrs. George D. Morgan ("George and Oyuki" to the Newport set) crossed the Pacific and arrived in Portland, Oregon, George's birthplace. Night after night, balls and receptions were held in her honor. Fireworks lit the night sky. Then came a one-year honeymoon in Paris, after which the couple settled down in France until Morgan's death in 1913.

Her Morgan in-laws were compassionate and saw to it that Oyuki was able to live in comfort, but without her husband at her side she failed to find contentment or happiness anywhere she tried to live.

Oyuki the geisha.
*Courtesy of Mainichi Newspaper*

Making a final pilgrimage to George's grave, Oyuki knelt and vowed that her love for him would know no end. She then returned to Japan and lodged herself once more in Kyoto. It was now 1938, just when relations between her native country and her adopted land were beginning to sour.

Oyuki quickly learned she would have fared better had she stayed in the United States or France. In Japan, her identity documents were questioned. Less support came from the Morgans, and she began to sell some of her treasured possessions. In Japan, though, she was widely believed to be a woman of untold resources and was continually petitioned to make one philanthropic gesture or another. Pleas for money poured in by mail. Other mendicants waited with open palms outside her home. Suspecting she might be a spy, the dreaded thought police opened her mail. She had to employ a maid-servant to help her ward off unwelcome intruders. (Eventually she adopted the maid legally.) Whenever she went out, Oyuki hid behind a black veil.

With each passing year the aging Oyuki retreated deeper into seclusion. The less that was known about her daily life, the more bizarre the rumors that were spread about her: she became a hopeless alcoholic, she never bathed, she lived hand-to-mouth on the meager earnings of her adopted daughter (the maid-servant).

In 1951 the writer Kazuo Kikuta composed a comic opera about her called *Morgan Oyuki* that was quite successful. How much, if any, money Oyuki received is not known.

On May 20, 1963, Oyuki Morgan died of pneumonia at her home in Kita Ward, Kyoto. She was 81.

As NOTED, the *shira-byoshi* of the late twelfth century were forerunners of modern geisha. They were troubadours who traveled from fief to fief, castle to castle, market-town to market-town, dressed all in white with long, voluminous sleeves. Their performances included epic ballads, ancient poems and dramatized accounts of clan conflicts and the high deeds (to pass all believing) of *daimyo*, samurai, and *ronin*. These women committed their entire repertoire to memory, thereby serving as living repositories of myths, legends, and the usual deceptions with which history is rife.

By the mid-sixteenth century, the word "geisha" began to appear in extant records, most often as *machi-geisha*, or "geisha of the town or streets." These women were in truth street-walkers and were considered even lower in class than the *yuna*, or bathhouse prostitutes. (What wondrous places the sixteenth-century bathhouses must have been, to have had prostitutes installed on the premises alongside the *sansuke*, men who lived by scrubbing the backs of bathers.)

Oyuki, the former geisha, after marrying George D. Morgan.

*Courtesy of UPI/Corbis Bettmann*

In the seventeenth century the geisha took a long stride forward toward their present image by becoming performers whose job it was to keep customers entertained while waiting for the *oiran* (the *crème de la crème* of Yoshiwara harlotry) to appear and take over. Because these haughty Yoshiwara courtesans would brook no sexual competition, the geisha of their day were forced to rely more and more on their music and dancing to earn a living. As the popularity of the *oiran* declined, that of the geisha rose until the geisha became superior symbols of status who were qualified to marry even prime ministers and the scions of noble families.

From the time of the Meiji Restoration until the end of the war in the Pacific, the geisha were in the full bloom of their development. The concentration of diverse political forces in Tokyo, the widening distribution of affluence, the modernization of the nation under influences from abroad, and the deterioration of their elaborate licensed quarters combined to form the backdrop against which the geisha could act out their moments on the stage as the companions—and sometimes the manipulators—of rich, famous, and influential men.

During the first three-quarters of the twentieth century, the training of a geisha achieved a high standard never before or after realized. In fact, it was believed that to become truly accomplished in the essential arts of samisen playing, singing, and posture dancing could require as long as thirty years. By then the geisha would be fifty years old at least and have the physical appearance of a *rakan* (skin-and-bones Buddhist ascetics such as are to be found among the *genro geisha* ("elder statesman" geisha) who are looked upon with respect—but seldom lust—at important social functions.

Impoverished rural families were usually the source of apprentice geisha, who might be sold to a *geisha-ya* when they were only five or six. In part, that custom explains the dearth of great beauties among these courtesans since most were tapped for candidacy at an undeveloped age when it was difficult to predict how their features and figures might mature.

The training lasted from five to ten years, depending on when the apprenticeship began, and often included attendance at a neighborhood school. Otherwise, tutors were called in for it was vital that the geisha be able to read and write as well as to know something of history, literature, and current events. More than a few would be expected in later years to speak intelligently and entertainingly to some of the sharper minds in the country, many of whom chose the geisha to grace their parties as carefully as a bon vivant selects his wines.

Even so, lessons in singing (they were once commonly called "singing-girls"), dancing, and the samisen took priority, for these were the basic tools of the trade. Housed in the *geisha-ya* under the supervision of the manageress who held their contracts, they led simple—but not necessarily spartan—lives. Contrary to what more lurid imaginations might expect, a deliberate effort was made to protect these young girls from foreknowledge of the seamier side of geisha existence—simply because apparent naiveté in *maiko* or *hangyoku* (apprentice geisha) was highly prized and because such manifest pristine innocence at the time of the girl's "debut" could enable the manageress to partly or wholly recoup her investment.

In time, each apprentice was assigned to a full-fledged geisha of the house, to run errands for her and assist in her time-consuming daily rituals of bathing and dressing and to enable the apprentice to absorb knowledge by watching and listening. When she was judged ready, she became a *hangyoku* ("half-jewel") or *maiko* (as they are known in Kyoto) and entered the demanding, dazzling world of the geisha.

At about seventeen, the *hangyoku's* moment-of-truth arrives. She first decides what she will call herself for the remainder of her professional life and chooses the name from among such odd sobriquets as Kosode (Little Sleeve), Osome (Honorable Dyeing), Ponta (phonetic; no particular meaning), and Kosen (Little Hermit).

Armed with her new name, she and her manageress set out on her *o-hirome*, or debut. They call at each of the restaurants that might eventually avail themselves of her services to introduce her and leave small presents. Shortly thereafter comes the *mizuage-shiki*, or the defloration ceremony itself, which is quite important for the geisha's future welfare and prosperity.

The more influential and affluent her despoiler, the better this augurs for her later popularity. Like the number of mistresses he keeps, the number of geisha he has deflowered is a consequential ingredient in the formation of one's reputation for machismo in Japan.

Further, to become known as a man about town in the world of geisha, it is generally accepted that one must spend at least ten evenings every month in a restaurant with geisha in attendance and must run up a monthly bill from such activities of at least five million yen...both for one year.

After defloration, the geisha adopts more conservative, but nonetheless expensive, attire and more mature hairstyling, then settles down to her life's work. She may have several patrons at the same time or she may become attached early to one patron who will sooner or later take her out of the world of the *mizu-shobai* (the water-business, so called because the players flow in and out like water) or she may go through extended periods without any patrons at all. And she may have isolated sexual encounters without any regard to the existence of a patron. Perhaps in reaction to the life she leads, she may enter into a relationship (which probably is—but need not be—sexual) with a man entirely unrelated to her way of life: a cook, perhaps, or a teacher.

For reasons of convenience and economy, she will continue to live under the roof of her manageress, at least as long as she is in that woman's debt. Because most geisha parties are over by ten o'clock or so, she is able to bed down—alone or in company—comparatively early and thus rise in the mornings long before her spiritual sisters of the cabaret, bar, and night-club circuit.

Her mornings are filled with lessons: flower arrangement, tea ceremony, dancing, samisen, and so forth. After a simple lunch—usually brought in from a nearby *demae* restaurant, she relaxes and chatters with other geisha until about three o'clock, when she begins to beautify herself for the evening: facials with rice-bran (nightingale dung is said to be the best but is quite costly), light hair shaved from wherever it is excessive or unsightly, skin bracing with dried gourds, hard skin removed from the feet with pumice, the public bath, milk lotion for the face and neck, hair styling, the application of white powder to the nape of the neck, and finally the donning of the kimono and the tying of the obi.

Until quite recently, the financial affairs of the geisha were strictly controlled, mostly by persons other than the geisha herself and generally to her disadvantage. It was her custom to go from her quarters in the early evening to the *kemban*, or geisha call-office, where she received her assignment slip. From there she rode in a rickshaw to her first *o-zashiki* (where the dinners are held) of the evening. (The few rickshaws still in business in Japan are those that specialize in carrying geisha. It is an eye-catching contrast to see those two-wheeled, coolie-drawn conveyances of by-gone days pull up to the fashionable *o-zashiki* of Shimbashi and Akasaka to fraternize with the long, black limousines of politicians and stalwarts of the commercial and financial communities.)

After leaving the party, the geisha would ask someone in the *o-zashiki* to sign her slip testifying to the length of time she shared her wit and charm with the guests. At the end of the month, the *kemban* billed the restaurant that in turn billed the host of the party. Upon receipt of the

payment, the *kemban* deducted its fee as agent and forwarded the rest
to the person responsible for the geisha's finances. Depending on her
age, experience, popularity, extent of indebtness, and other factors, each
geisha made her own contractual arrangements with her manageress.

Nowadays the geisha is considered an independent businesswoman.
She is fully protected from exploitation by labor regulations and must
be eighteen years old in order to become a full-fledged entertainer.
While the older women may still ride to work in rickshaws, the
younger ones may go on scooters—or even drive their own cars.

Armless nun Junkyo, formerly the geisha Tsuma-kichi, age seventy-five.

*Courtesy of Bukko-in, Kyoto*

Instead of devoting their mornings to lessons in the tea ceremony or
floral arrangement, many practice golf or visit their stock-broker. In
lieu of years of arduous training, a woman may decide that she wants
to be an "instant geisha," register herself with a *kemban* for ¥30,000—
and lo! be established in business. Of course, the higher-class districts
will insist on some proof of ability in the traditional geisha arts, but
others may be satisfied with only her physical presence, especially if
she is attractive, and initiation fee.

It is in the high-class *o-zashiki* that the movers and shakers of Japan gather to discuss and plan political upheavals and financial coups. Here they can enjoy atmospheres of trust and intimacy, to a degree impossible in offices, public restaurants, or homes. Aside from the actual participants in these machinations, the geisha are the only ones present and they come to be leaned on more than wives or employees or other outsiders would be.

In the troublous times after the restoration of the Emperor Meiji in 1868, the centers of political power and intrigue shifted with alarming alacrity. The clique in power or favor today might be in utter disarray and confusion on the morrow. In such conditions, many politicians found their favorite geisha to be oases of calm and stability. Indeed, they often came to rely on the geisha for even more: for financing, for loyalty, and for confidential information.

Three men who later rose to the highest political office in Japan—that of prime minister—married their faithful geisha, probably in appreciation of their loyalty and assistance: Hirobumi Ito, Taro Katsura, and Aritomo Yamagata. Their geisha-wives were Koume, O-Koi, and Oimatsu.

Other leaders of Japan who either married a geisha or lived with one in a state bordering on marriage included Takamori Saigo, Kimmochi Saionji, Koin Kido, Tsuyoshi Inukai, Shigeru Yoshida, Shojiro Goto, Kaoru Inoue, Genzui Kusaka, Keisuke Okada, and Munemitsu Mutsu—all names to be reckoned with.

THE LAST IN THE LIST—Count Munemitsu Mutsu—was Ambassador to the U.S. and later foreign minister. I have seen a photograph of his wife Kosuzu of Shimbashi and must say she was an extraordinarily handsome woman.

A striking combination of intelligence, beauty, and savoir-faire, this woman has been praised by many aficionados as the "greatest of all geisha." She went by the unlikely name of O-Koi-san, or Miss Honorable Carp, a fish greatly admired for the courage and tenacity it displays when fighting against the current of a river.

Miss Carp had been sold at the age of six to a teahouse owner to be trained as a geisha.

Tall for a Japanese, she immediately became popular after making her debut at sixteen. Four years later she was married to a well-known kabuki actor but divorced him when she was twenty-four, to return to her life as a geisha.

Her big chance came when she was selected to be the lead geisha in a group of fifty of her colleagues. Their assignment was to provide the entertainment and camaraderie at a banquet to welcome a delegation from Russia. This was just prior to the outbreak of the Russo-Japanese War. Among those in attendance at the banquet was Prince Taro Katsura of the Imperial family, who was also prime minister of Japan.

Smitten with O-Koi-san, the Prince lost no time in declaring his intent to have her as his mistress. She promptly moved into appropriate quarters within shouting distance of Katsura's official residence.

Despite the binational friendship that had prevailed at the fifty-geisha banquet, Japan and Russia opened hostilities and fell on each other tooth and nail in a war remembered for a splendid naval victory, the copious shedding of blood, and treachery most vile. (For instance, the Japanese offered three Russian officers the sum of no less than $65 million for the plans to the fortifications of a vital defensive position at Port Arthur. A deal was struck. Using the secret plans, the Japanese under General Maresuke Nogi attacked and overran the targeted hill. After the cessation of hostilities, the three Russian officers met the Japanese at an agreed-upon location in Europe to collect their reward. They disappeared from the face of the earth thereafter.)

Anyway, Japan had won the war—the first time an Oriental power had defeated a European country—hands down, but her spoils from the conflict were so trifling that outrage swept across Japan. Prince Katsura was accused of having sold out his country. He and his mistress were badgered and humiliated publicly.

At length, Katsura decided he had no choice but to announce he would give up his post as prime minister—and abandon his mistress. (How the Japanese public figured that O-Koi-san had anything to do with the peace negotiations in Portsmouth is mystifying, like much else in public life, but she bowed and went gracefully.)

When the hubbub had died away, the Prince retired to his country villa and ensconced O-Koi-san in an abode close at hand, later making theirs a licit union.

When at length Katsura died, Miss Carp tried her hand at running a Ginza bar, which proved to be not so successful, prompting her to return to the "flower and willow" world as the operator of a teahouse in a geisha district.

Even the teahouse did not meet her expectations so she shaved her still-lovely head and joined an order of Buddhist nuns.

At the age of seventy, in 1948, O-Koi-san died in her sleep.

### References

1.  Deighton, Len. *Blood, Tears and Folly*. New York: Harper Collins, 1993.

2.  Enright, D.J. *The World of Dew*. Tokyo: Charles E. Tuttle, 1956.

3.  Santaro. "Between Geisha and Harlot." *Asahi Evening News* (Tokyo), November 8, 1958.

4.  "Oyuki Morgan Leads Lonely Life." *Yomiuri Japan News* (Tokyo), August 12, 1957.

5.  Wheeler, Post, and Hallie Erminie Rides. *Dome of Many-Colored Glass*, Garden City: Doubleday, 1975.

# CHAPTER EIGHT
# Children at War

*It is not that the Japanese don't love their children. Usually parents protect—even overprotect—them until they are well into their twenties. But the imperatives of war betimes demand unusual sacrifice, heedless of age.*

## THE WHITE TIGER BAND

### AIZU-WAKAMATSU 1868

The youngsters, all sons of samurai, had retreated to a position on Mount Iimori from where they could discern Tsurugajo (Crane Castle) in the distance. This citadel was the stronghold of their Lord Katamori Matsudaira and was enveloped in smoke. They conferred briefly.

"The castle has fallen," said one in a still immature voice.

Another: "That means our Lord is either dead or has been captured."

"Never!" spoke up a third, a near-midget. "He would never allow himself to be captured."

"Anyway," said their leader, the boy with the sad eyes, "we know what we must do now."

They all nodded in solemn affirmation.

The graceful lines of the castle were said to have reminded many of a crane in flight. The soaring structure stood in Aizu-Wakamatsu, seat of the Aizu domain of that branch of the Matsudaira family. (This is now the western part of Fukushima Prefecture, well north of Tokyo.)

The Matsudairas were among the most steadfast myrmidons of the House of Tokugawa, and around their castle was fought in 1868 one of the last battles of the Boshin-no-eki (Boshin War), whose issue was restoration of full hegemony to the Emperor (Meiji) and unseating of the Tokugawa Shogun. Inside the castle were the diminutive Lord Katamori Matsudaira and a small part of his considerable army while investing it were the Imperial forces.

It was to be a ferocious fight, for the Aizu samurai had the reputation of being among the toughest in feudal Japan. As samurai, the Aizu men swore by the code of Bushido, the quintessence of which is "Bushido is the way of dying." So simple, so easy to say. This belief was not unique to Aizu, of course. All Japanese samurai were solemnly bound to awaken every morning with the stern self-admonition to be prepared to meet their fate before the sun set that evening.

But Aizu boasted the Nisshinkan, one of the five best schools in the nation and an academy where the martial arts and the precepts of the Warrior Code were emphasized above all else. Like all samurai children in Aizu, the boys in the White Tiger Band had been schooled there from the age of six.

One of the textbooks at the school taught the student, "Love others, not yourself. It is most disloyal and unfilial to covet the pleasures of life, to love yourself, and not to do that which you should do."

An Aizu-bred general who later served in the Russo-Japanese War (1904–5) wrote in his autobiography, "...from the age of six I was given the training and education unique to Aizu. I was taught the way of loyalty, faithfulness, filial piety, and obedience."

In March 1868, Lord Matsudaira began to make preparations to fend off incursions into his domain of Aizu by the forces of the new Imperial government. Since his intrepid samurai had always been under arms, he now laid plans to conscript townsmen and farmers, grouped by age.

Some were called by such oddly unmilitary names as the Black Turtle Corps and the Red Sparrow Corps, others by more martial nomenclature: the Blue Dragon Corps and the White Tiger Corps (all sixteen and seventeen in age). These were names of creatures associated with the gods of the four cardinal points.

The anti-Shogunal forces began to advance north that summer, other castles falling to their irresistible tide—with some bases surrendering after only token resistance. In August these forces began to gird their loins for an all-out assault on the nerve center of what was called the Northern League: Aizu-Wakamatsu.

Aizu lay in a basin encircled by formidable mountains. It was through the passes between these peaks that the Imperial army would have to come if they were to invade Aizu. The Imperial staff determined to make use of an early form of military disinformation. They spread word that their battalions would penetrate the mountains through Nakayama Pass, the shortest route. Deceived by the rumor, Matsudaira shifted his regiments to reinforce that pass while leaving other routes dangerously short of much needed defenders. As one might expect, the Emperor Meiji's phalanxes poured through elsewhere: the sparsely defended Bonari Pass on August 21.

The situation was grave; Matsudaira had fewer than one thousand men in reserve back at the Crane Castle with which to seal off the gap. Normally he would not have considered dispatching the White Tiger boys to the front lines. Not only were they children but he looked upon them as the future leaders of the Aizu clan.

While pondering this urgent situation, the boys themselves—thirty-seven of them remained in the castle—began to plead that Matsudaira let them go. When at length he relented, they shouted and cried with joy. Off they went, enthusiastic to test their blades and see what fate had in store for them—if, as budding samurai, they could indeed "die before sunset."

Their first encounter with the foe was at a bridge vital to the protection of their domain. The more numerous government soldiers crossed the bridge with ease but were brought to a halt by darkness. Having received reinforcements during the night, the Emperor's squadrons sortied with fresh vigor the next morning. The Aizu men, including the White Tiger boys, were mauled severely in the engagement.

Falling back, the surviving twenty White Tigers decided to return to Crane Castle and lay down their lives defending Lord Matsudaira. En route they ran into another strong detachment of the government troops and in their withdrawal were forced to seek refuge on the forested slopes of nearby Mount Iimori.

From a coign near the top of the mountain, the tenacious survivors could dimly see their beloved castle in the distance. Smoke and flames shrouded the structure that so resembled a flying crane. To the White Tiger Band, this could only mean that all was lost.

Cemetery in Aizu-Wakamatsu where members of the White Tiger Band are buried. *Courtesy of Mihir Sapru*

Thereupon the remnants of the Band unsheathed their short swords and unhesitatingly disemboweled themselves or stabbed themselves in the throat. (Actually, three of the members cut open their abdomens a slight distance apart from the others. Also, one—Yuji Nagase—had to be decapitated by a comrade because he was immobile, having been wounded by rifle fire in the stomach. And still another survived by a mysterious twist of fate.)

The White Tiger youths had been a trifle precipitous. The castle had not fallen. The flames and smoke seen at a distance rose from nearby samurai residences set aflame by the government soldiery. The Aizu domain did not surrender until November 6.

Not until the following spring was a concerted search made for the White Tigers. Their nineteen bodies had been covered by winter's blanket of snow, hampering their discovery. When at last they were found, ravens had pecked away most of the flesh, leaving only skeletonized remains. The cemetery where they were laid to rest is often visited by members of the public who know of the boys' courage and loyalty to the Aizu cause and who want to wish their spirits well.

## THE STAR LILY CORPS

### OKINAWA 1945

At least 150,000 Okinawa noncombatants died during the battle that began on that island in March 1945. Of that number 167 were girls—sixteen and seventeen in age—who either committed suicide or were killed by American shells and bullets. A book (*Himeyuri no To*) has been written about them and from this a movie was made.

The Himeyuri Memorial was erected near the cave where many of these girls died. One of their teachers dedicated a short poem to them, which was engraved on the face of the memorial. In English, it read, "Stones make hard pillows, but I pray you rest in peace."

Of the 167, there were 155 who had been enrolled in the elite Himeyuri (Star Lily, or Princess Lily) Girls' School, so strict in its separation of the sexes that to exchange even a word with a boy was grounds for expulsion.

These patriotic girls volunteered to suspend their studies and join the Student Medical Corps, but before they could help treat any of the flood of wounded, the medical facilities to which they were to be assigned were destroyed in an air raid. In hope of achieving enhanced safety for the injured and ailing, the Japanese army caused twenty-one caves to be dug into the face of a low hill near Haebaru. The idea was sound, but there was no time to dig connecting tunnels, hence no cross-ventilation in the caves. American shelling had halted further excavation.

The caves were designated as wards for certain kinds of injuries or illnesses. (One ward for tuberculosis, the next for surgery, a third for general medicine, and so forth.) They turned out to be wretched pits of agony for the sick and hurt and for those trying to relieve their suffering.

In his excellent book *Tennozan*, American author George Feifer presents the story of seventeen-year-old Ruriko Morishita, one of the older and most patriotic of the nurses' aides. She was one of the few to survive this perdition on earth and was interviewed many years later by author Feifer about her experiences in what came to be called the Caves of the Virgins.

Visitors climbing steps to the cemetery to pay homage to members of the White Tiger Band. *Courtesy of Mihir Sapru*

Ruriko was given duty in Ward Three—a collection of a half-dozen caves for amoebic dysentery, typhoid, malaria, and tuberculosis. Ward Three quickly overflowed with patients. Except to fetch food, water, and supplies, the nurses' aides could not leave the jam-packed, dark caves and had to sleep cheek to jowl with the sick (and injured, for Ward Three could no longer be set aside for infectious diseases only).

Candles became the only illumination in the caves, but these soon guttered due to lack of oxygen. Water dripped from ceilings on patients and medical staff alike. Evil odors from sweat, urine, blood, pus, and feces made Ruriko try not to breathe at all. Lice from the soldiers transferred their attentions to the upper-class girls.

Monument in Itoman, Okinawa that commemorates the war-time sacrifices of the girls in the Star Lily Corps. *Courtesy of Mainichi Newspaper*

Maggots crawled around in open wounds. Their busy chewing could be heard throughout the grim nights, driving even the most intrepid around the bend. Believing that the maggots warded off tetanus by consuming pus from the wounds, the girls tried not to disturb them. Ruriko, however, had to pick many of the worms off with a pair of chopsticks when they were dining near the mouth of a wounded soldier, lest too many fall down his throat.

Ruriko was kept busy helping to carry recently dead bodies or amputated limbs to the mouth of her cave. When Japanese soldiers passed out hand grenades to the medical staff for purposes of self-immolation, Ruriko fondled hers as if it were a blessing from on high. Wherever she went next, even if it were on to the fields of brimstone and fire, it would be like Takamagahara (the Japanese paradise) compared to where she now existed.

For a cloistered youngster like Ruriko Morishita, among her most difficult moments were those when she was required to help half-dead strangers achieve bowel movements and to grasp the *dankon* (penises) to direct the urine streams of soldiers whose arms were in casts or were amputated. Or when the pitiable, suffering men sprayed her with noisome, maggot-filled vomitus.

At the end something exploded just within the mouth of Ruriko's cave. Those near the explosion could not breathe in the thick white smoke and assumed they were being suffocated by poison gas.

As the smoke (probably from white phosphorous hand grenades) penetrated deeper into the cave's interior, a half-dead male orderly advised the aides to urinate on their trousers (they wore shapeless, uniform-like clothing) and breathe through the wet cloth. This tactic apparently enabled the petite, chaste Miss Morishita to survive. When she could at last exit the cave, she crawled down a ditch where she was shot three times by American soldiers. (She later doubted the enemy could distinguish she was a girl, she was so covered with mud and assorted filth.)

An aide lying beside her—a friend from school—pulled out her hand grenade and extracted the pin.

Ruriko had never welcomed anything more than the demise she believed to be on the point of embracing her, but the grenade was to be a dud. By then a squad of Americans was standing over her. In a bloody daze, she finally understood that these "cruel barbarians" were trying to help her.

In addition to 155 members of the Star Lily Corps, more than one thousand teenage boys conscripted for auxiliary service also had their young lives taken in those final days of the campaign on Okinawa.

### References

1.  Feifer, George. *Tennozan* (The Battle of Okinawa and the Atom Bomb). New York: Ticknor & Fields, 1981.

2. Warner, Dennis, and Peggy Warner. *The Sacred Warriors: Japan's Suicide Legions*. New York: Avon Books, 1982.

3. "The White Tiger Band." *The East* (Tokyo), November–December 1995.

4. Suzuki Kenji. *Rekishi e no Shotai* (An Invitation to History), Vol. 14. Tokyo: Nippon Hoso Shuppon Kyokai, 1983.

5. *Kodansha Encyclopedia of Japan*. Tokyo: Kodansha International, 1983.

## Chapter Nine

# One or Two Dozen
# Tokyo Roses

⟨ornament⟩

*In 1949, in the state of California, an American woman was tried and convicted of treason, mostly owing to the fact that Japanese blood ran through her veins. By 1995 the national mood had changed to the extent that when a rich black man who loved white women was tried for murders he almost certainly committed, a racist jury set him free and thumbed their noses at the majority of Americans who believed him to be as guilty as sin.*

### San Francisco 1949

It was a strange and tragic proceeding that took place in San Francisco in 1949. On trial was not so much a Japanese–American woman named Iva Ikuko Toguri d'Aquino but rather a myth—a myth who, because of war-engendered hatreds, had become both a *bête noire* and the focus of fascinated misconceptions.

This myth went by the name of "Tokyo Rose." The difference between the myth and the stocky, rather plain Miss Iva Toguri was, as the Japanese would say, like the difference between the moon and a tortoise. Miss Toguri herself was aware of this difference. She said of her early interviewers, "They expected to see Ava Gardner but instead found only me."

Even before MacArthur had landed at Atsugi, early-bird American correspondents were racing here and there in the Tokyo–Yokohama area looking for the mythical Tokyo Rose, whose sexy-voiced broadcasts had so "enraptured" Allied military personnel in the Pacific Theater of war. The question of her whereabouts was asked over and over again, but almost no Japanese even knew who, much less where, she was.

How could this be? Tokyo Rose was a name almost as familiar to the American public as Tojo or Hirohito or even Hitler, Goering, or Goebbels. Personnel at Radio Tokyo, the presumed source of the so-called Tokyo Rose broadcasts, were uncertain which of many radio announcers might be most entitled to the mythical name.

It is not known who first assigned the name Tokyo Rose to the seductive temptress whose voice was heard by millions of GIs in their pup-tents and foxholes. Japan had seventeen radio stations throughout the Pacific, and of these a total of twenty-seven women had made broadcasts in English for American ears.

After the war a few American veterans of the Pacific war swore they had heard English-language broadcasts made by a woman who called herself "Tokyo Rose." All such broadcasts were monitored and overtly recorded (I heard them in our Japanese language school in 1945), and no recording has ever been found that verifies the veterans' recollections.

In fact, few of the announcers identified themselves by any name. The cult of the individual did not apply in Japan, then or now. Miss Toguri was a rare exception. Sometimes she called herself "Orphan Ann" or "Orphan Annie."

Her supervisor and voice coach at Radio Tokyo gave her that name. The "Ann" came from the abbreviation "Ann." for "Announcer," which identified her voice parts on the scripts. On the radio Miss Toguri had been calling her GI audience "orphans of the Pacific," and when her coach Major Cousens learned of the popular American comic strip "Little Orphan Annie," that settled it. Orphan Ann (or Annie) it was to be. But never Tokyo Rose.

Nevertheless, American radio broadcasts were monitored in Tokyo by the Domei News Agency, so toward the latter part of the war those selected few who read the Domei transcripts became aware that the name "Tokyo Rose" had earned considerable currency among Americans. But no announcer was ever identified in their minds as Tokyo Rose.

In August 1945 the regal *New York Times* had reported the results of a study done by the Office of War Information: "There is no Tokyo Rose; the name is strictly a GI invention.... Government monitors listening in twenty-four hours a day have never heard the (name) Tokyo Rose over a Japanese-controlled radio (broadcast)...."

But while Tokyo Rose lived mostly in the imagination, Iva Toguri existed in the flesh—a petite woman of thirty with a somewhat square face and a gravely, almost masculine voice not suited to enrapturing the "Orphans of the Pacific." ("Orphans" came from an idea the Japanese wanted to promote: that the American forces in the Pacific had been largely abandoned by the people back home. The U.S. administration wanted to win the war in Europe first, while American wives and sweethearts were more concerned with the mundane pleasures immediately available to them.)

It was her voice that first caught the attention of Major Charles Hughes Cousens when he found Iva in the Radio Tokyo typists' pool. Hers was an unusual voice, and he liked that. It was also what he called a "gin fog voice," and he liked that, too. What he wanted was a "comedy voice," for it was his intent to sabotage the Japanese propaganda broadcasts that he was being coerced to plan and supervise. He had to correct some of Iva's poor speech habits and her rapid chattering style. Cousens had been the Walter Cronkite of news announcers in Australia and spoke beautiful English in the Sandhurst manner. (Of course, he had attended Sandhurst.)

Many long hours of effort paid off, and Iva's harsh, throaty speech became more lively and gay and, yes, somewhat comical. The many other women who broadcast from Radio Tokyo in English spoke, for the most part, in sweet, pleasant voices. Iva's newly acquired vocal style was not exactly unpleasant, but it was different. It was now a voice that would be remembered. And that was what Cousens wanted.

A few years later, in 1946, I was visiting the country home of Ruth Hayakawa on the banks of the Chikugo River in central Kyushu.

Unknown to me at the time was the fact that Ruth had been one of the women who had broadcast in English from Radio Tokyo. In fact, Ruth had substituted for Iva on Sunday evenings when Iva was not working.

One afternoon Ruth was in the kitchen helping her mother with dinner. She had left me in the *osetsuma* (living area) with a brown, label-less bottle of good Japanese beer, a hand-wound gramophone, and a stack of 78-rpm records. Most of them were pre-war American songs, but I found one among them with a hand-written label on it reading "Maj. Cousens." It was a recording of the Australian major who was found neither innocent nor guilty in an Australian court of charges of treason, giving voice lessons to Ruth.

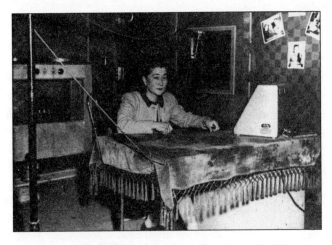

Iva Toguri, known as "Tokyo Rose" broadcasting to Allied Forces.
*Courtesy of UPI/Corbis-Bettmann*

She walked into the room while the record was still playing. "An Australian friend of mine gave me voice lessons," she explained. I thought no more about it at the time, but remembered that record and Ruth's comment much later when I learned she had been one of the many women who might have qualified as Tokyo Rose. (Ruth Hayakawa was later elected to the Japanese Diet.) To her credit, Miss

Hayakawa testified that she had never heard Iva Toguri broadcast anything detrimental to the interests of the United States.

In any event, the plain, small, square-faced Iva Toguri was no slinky, silky-voiced, sexy seductress. As Iva herself said, Ava Gardner she was not. But there was one of the twenty-seven radio broadcasters who personified the mythical image much more closely. Her name was Myrtle Lipton, and she had become known as "Manila Rose."

Miss Lipton was part American, part Filipino. She was five-feet-five and had lovely legs and a golden complexion. Her voice was that of a torch singer, low and a little husky. It was a charming voice, but her physical presence was, if anything, even more appealing. She had captivated many Americans, both in the Philippines and in Singapore. Her "Manila Rose" programs were modeled after the Zero Hour broadcasts from Tokyo—and also one called the German Hour.

After the war, Myrtle Lipton was summoned in Manila for interrogation by the U.S. Army Counter-Intelligence Corps (C.I.C.) with an FBI representative present. This beautiful, charming woman broke down in tears when questioned about her propaganda broadcasts for the Japanese. The C.I.C. interrogating officer took pity on this lachrymose, winsome creature and released her from custody. Although she had been listed as a collaborator and although there was a twelve-page file on her, the C.I.C. declared its investigation closed. Shortly thereafter, Miss Lipton disappeared. No trace of her has ever been found. Her name is not found in the files of the Counter-Intelligence Corps, where it obviously should be.

If the American journalists and other investigators in Tokyo had discovered Myrtle Lipton instead of Iva ("I'm no Ava Gardner") Toguri, they might have reported that verisimilitude and fantasy were, for once, close kin to each other. It was almost as if they decided to take it out on poor little Iva Toguri for not being Myrtle Lipton—or Ava Gardner.

BACK IN TOKYO, in the final days of August and the early days of September, our pack of enterprising foreign correspondents was baying in full voice on the trail of one of their top assigned targets—Tokyo

Rose. Inevitably, Iva Toguri and her Portuguese husband Filipe d'Aquino learned of the search. Iva did not understand that they were searching avidly for a traitor going by the appellation Tokyo Rose. She believed they wanted to interview a famous female announcer known abroad by that name. She must have dreamed of fame and perhaps even fortune. After all, she was now unemployed and practically without money. Her husband warned her against getting involved, but she could see no harm in it. If her fellow Americans wanted to think of her as Tokyo Rose, why, let them. She had, after all, made some silly propaganda broadcasts as Orphan Ann, but there was no intended harm in them.

Iva was located in early September 1945 by correspondents Clark Lee and Harry Brundidge, of INS and *Cosmopolitan*, respectively. They asked her if she was really Tokyo Rose. Iva made the very major mistake of hesitating, then saying yes, perhaps thinking of the fame and fortune soon to follow (and not a trial for treason). Brundidge offered her $2,000 for an exclusive interview with his magazine, *Cosmopolitan*. He drew up a contract (Miss Toguri never received any money from Brundidge or from *Cosmopolitan* and typed in her name "Iva Ikuko Toguri (Tokyo Rose)."

Earlier Iva had denied that identity, stating she was no more Tokyo Rose than any of the other twenty-six women who had broadcast in English on Japanese radio. Now here she was signing a contract specifying that Tokyo Rose was her other identity. Why?

One of the two correspondents present at the fateful signing, Clark Lee of INS, believed the answer was vanity, and nothing more. He later wrote that she must have been thinking, "I am an international figure known to millions of American GIs and sailors. I have become world famous. My story will be in nearly every paper in America.… My picture will be everywhere."

Ah, vanity. We humans can be cured, it is said, of every folly but vanity.

Iva Toguri was in high spirits. Her country had won the war and now she had become the popular and famous Tokyo Rose—an idol of sorts to GIs and sailors. Little did she suspect that the *Los Angeles Examiner* would carry on September 3, 1945, a front-page story identifying her as one Iva Ikuko Toguri, a graduate of UCLA—and a traitor.

From then until her treason trial in 1949 must have been, for Iva Toguri, a trying and mystifying period. The U.S. Department of Justice had declined to charge her with treason, saying there was insufficient evidence to do so. She was interrogated, held in custody, followed around by GIs wanting her to autograph their Japanese paper money with the name Tokyo Rose, imprisoned in Sugamo for almost one year, and hounded for interviews.

American correspondents interview Iva Toguri in September 1945.
*Courtesy of the National Archives*

Her Portuguese husband Filipe d'Aquino persisted in his advice that she drop out of sight and later return to her home in the U.S. as quietly as she could. Unfortunately, she did not take his advice (or perhaps it was already too late to do so.) She could even have shared in her husband's Portuguese citizenship (and placed herself out of the reaches of the U.S. government and a vengeful American society), but she thought of herself as a red, white, and blue American wanting nothing more than to go back home. Throughout this period and even during the subsequent treason trial, Miss Toguri had been sustained by one dominant thought. She would tell nothing but the truth and depend on her country's sense of justice to see her through.

Ruth Hayakawa, one of the twenty-seven women known as "Tokyo Rose" in Fukuoka, Japan, 1946

IVA IKUKO TOGURI was born in Los Angeles on July 4, 1916 (an ironic birth date for traitor-to-be Iva), to parents Jun and Fumi Toguri. Iva was, of course a U.S. citizen by birth. Her father also had her birth recorded in his *koseki* (family register) in Japan. This gave her dual nationality. This situation continued until January 1932 when her father decided to have her name removed from the register in Japan. Many other Japanese immigrants were doing the same to allay burgeoning suspicions about dual citizenship. From the age of 16, Iva had only U.S. citizenship—until she lost it upon being convicted of treason. (She regained it when President Gerald Ford pardoned her in 1977.)

Iva's upbringing in California was thoroughly American. Her parents had deliberately tried to avoid living among clusters of other Japanese-

Americans. They tried to speak as little Japanese as possible, at least not to their children. They had become Christians and attended a Christian church regularly. Iva's playmates were nearly all Caucasians. She joined the Girl Scouts, took piano lessons, and played tennis, badminton, and field hockey. She was an ardent fan of movie actor James Stewart.

In 1934, she entered college to study zoology. Her college classmates would remember her as outgoing, lively, humorous, and energetic—a "completely average American girl." In 1940 she registered as a member of the Republican party. This was the same year she graduated from UCLA. She went on to graduate school, intending to become a doctor.

But in June, 1941 her aunt Shizu in Japan became quite ill. Iva's mother Fumi, who was diabetic and sickly, could not respond to Shizu's distress call, so the family decided that Iva, much against her wishes, would have to go to Japan instead.

She applied for a passport. There should have been no difficulty, for she was born in the U.S. and had never been out of the country. But the Department of State, widely known for its obfuscatory, dilatory ways, mysteriously delayed issuance of the document. Iva was told that if she had to go to Japan, she would have to travel on a "certificate of identification."

At this point Iva Toguri should have thrown up her hands in dismay and refused to budge, but that was not her way. She boarded the steamship bound for Japan, a country she had never visited. She knew not its language nor customs. She did not like Japanese food. (In fact, she carried thirty pieces of luggage, mostly filled with American foodstuffs. The thought of eating rice three times daily thoroughly distressed her.)

In Japan, she found that she did not like the humidity or the smells or the crowded conditions. Nevertheless, she was determined to make the best of it. She enrolled in a language school, but she was already planning to return home as soon as she had done her duty by her Aunt Shizu.

Her father became just as eager for her to return. More clearly than Iva, Jun could see the war-clouds looming. When his daughter had been in Japan for only four months, he telegraphed her money and said, "Come back as soon as you can."

Iva tried, but the lack of a U.S. passport complicated matters and she missed boarding the *Tatsuta-maru* in Yokohama. Perhaps that was just as well. The ship was halfway across the Pacific when Admiral Isoroku Yamamoto's carriers raided Pearl Harbor. The *Tatsuta-maru* had to turn back to Japan.

Two days after Pearl Harbor, a Special Security plainclothesman (the first of a continuing stream of such gendarmes) called on Iva Toguri and advised her to apply for Japanese citizenship. She replied that that was out of the question. If they were suspicious of her, she went on, then they should intern her with all the other Americans still trapped in Japan. The policeman laughed and said as a woman with a Japanese face, he did not think she would be any danger to Japan. Besides, he acknowledged, there were at least 10,000 other Japanese-Americans in Japan, and Japan could not afford to intern them all.

Iva then applied through the Swiss Embassy for a U.S. passport, but the Department of State in Washington replied that there were questions about Iva Toguri's citizenship. And even if Iva had met the schedule to board the next repatriation vessel (going to Africa via Goa), she could not have bought a ticket. It looked as if she might have to remain in Japan throughout the war.

She needed money badly; she could no longer be a burden on her ailing aunt and uncle. She had to get a job, but her lack of knowledge of Japanese was a handicap. At last she found a position in the Monitoring Division of the Domei News Agency. She listened to and recorded English-language broadcasts, paying particular attention to the movements of Allied military units. Although helping the Japanese learn about Allied military movements would seem to be very questionable and possibly treasonous, it was not for this act for which she was eventually tried.

In June, 1943—One-and-a-half years after Pearl Harbor—Iva fell seriously ill and was hospitalized. When discharged she fell deeper into debt, so she set out in earnest to find a second job. The English-language *Nippon Times*, which was still being published for the benefit of

English-speaking Europeans and others, ran a help-wanted ad for English-speaking typists at Radio Tokyo. Iva applied and was taken on. The noose around her neck was drawing tighter.

The Zero Hour program from Radio Tokyo, as devised by Major Charles Hughes Cousens, was an evening broadcast, an hour or so in length, that featured popular American music (with some classical mixed in), chatter by an announcer, and messages from POWs to folks back home. It proved to be popular with Allied troops. Cousens had resisted producing this program but was threatened with violence if he did not accede. He was determined to sabotage the effectiveness of the program.

The chief purpose of these Radio Tokyo broadcasts was to make American GIs and sailors homesick. If Americans fighting in the Pacific could be distracted and weakened by homesickness, they might be less effective. Or so calculated the Japanese. Homesickness was the objective stressed over and over again by the Japanese in charge at Radio Tokyo.

If I have to do it, I will, thought Cousens, but he would do it in a way that would be counterproductive. Since the Japanese officers who would review program scripts were far less than perfect in their understanding of English, an experienced radio announcer like Cousens could surely find ways to defeat their propagandistic aims.

In 1944, he was seeking ways to improve the contents but reduce the effectiveness of his program, the Zero Hour, which had grown in popularity, according to captured Americans, when he found Iva Toguri in the typing pool in the same building. She had—or would have, with his coaching—the kind of voice he wanted. She was doubtful about becoming an announcer, but it would fatten her pay envelope, so she succumbed to the Australian's blandishments. The noose became tighter.

THE LENGTHY and expensive trial of Iva Toguri d'Aquino for treason began on July 5, 1949. It was the last such legal proceeding to be held in the U.S. for alleged acts of treason committed during World War II.

Eight charges called "Overt Acts" were made against Iva. She was found innocent of seven of the Overt Acts and guilty of only one. Many did not agree with the verdict, including the foreman of the jury, but there arose no national outcry of "Foul play!" as had arisen in the instances of Alger Hiss and the Rosenbergs.

Even so, the trial and verdict were, for the most part, a miscarriage of justice. In the introduction to a book entitled *Tokyo Rose, Orphan of the Pacific*, former ambassador to Japan Edwin O. Reischauer wrote, "there was certainly no single 'Tokyo Rose,' nor was any person ever discovered who had traitorously engaged in propaganda activities against the United States in the fashion attributed by some to 'Tokyo Rose.'"

During the time between the end of World War II and the beginning of the trial in San Francisco, authorities both in the Occupation forces and in Washington had declared there was no case against Iva Toguri. The Legal Section of SCAP decided that Iva Toguri was not Tokyo Rose, and questioned if indeed such a person had ever existed at all.

Colonel H.I.T. Creswell, commanding officer of the Counter-Intelligence Corps, told an American journalist, "We've had (Iva Toguri) in Sugamo Prison for months and now we find we have no solid evidence against her." But he added, "We don't dare release her, since the (media) would promptly jump on our backs."

The Assistant Attorney General sent a letter to the Attorney General a memo reading, "It is my opinion that Toguri's activities are not sufficient to warrant her prosecution for treason." The U.S. Attorney in Los Angeles, where at first it was thought the trial might be staged, agreed in a telegram, that stated, "We feel evidence inadequate. Recommend treason prosecution be declined."

What had happened? Had new evidence been uncovered? No. Had new witnesses come forth? No.

Upon release from nearly a year in Sugamo Prison (and having the charges against her dropped), Iva Toguri wanted nothing more than to go home. "Cool it," her husband Filipe told her in what may have been the best advice he ever gave anyone. He told his wife that no one had forgotten her, that the many who wished her harm were merely lying in wait to pounce.

But Iva did not heed Filipe's sage counsel. After all, she was a native-born American citizen. She had really done nothing wrong. She loved her country. She was free; there were no charges pending against her. Surely people had forgotten all about her. So she went to the U.S. Consulate and applied once more for her passport. Again the Department of State went into its comical dance routine of delay and equivocation. Procrastination followed obstruction.

In the meantime, the Army newspaper *Stars and Stripes* learned that Iva had applied for repatriation and carried this news item on August 1, 1947. The story was picked up by papers back home. The witch hunt began once more, this time with more fervor.

As the FBI agent, Frederick G. Tillman, who had investigated Iva Toguri earlier was to say, "(Iva) was stupid, and all her trouble came from her own stupidity."

Be that as it may, her Rubicon was crossed. There was no turning back.

Leading the pack in pursuit of Iva was the scandal-mongering, enormously influential radio commentator Walter Winchell. Yapping at his heels were such organizations as the American Legion, the Los Angeles City Council, and the Native Sons of the Golden West. To all of them Iva Toguri was a flaming traitor, and there were no doubts about that. They did not want her to be allowed to return to the place of her birth.

The U.S. Department of Justice had only a short while before declared there was no real evidence against this unfortunate Nisei woman, but now they reversed their field. After all, Walter Winchell and the American Legion were formidable opponents. Moreover, it was an election year (1948), and the President's popularity was at low ebb.

In an appeal for the votes of the flag-wavers, the Department of Justice made up its mind to prosecute a fairly large number of treason cases pending since the end of World War II. Iva Toguri's name would now be added to the list of those to be charged. It was an unconscionable abandonment of the principles of justice in the interests of political expediency.

The case against Iva Toguri was then, in the words of Edwin O. Reischauer, "pursued pantingly by journalists hungry for a scoop. It

was taken up by counter-intelligence officers and then by civil law officials more eager to prove themselves relentless bloodhounds on the
trail of malefactors than upholders of justice and the individual human
rights of which we are today so conscious. It was tolerated by politicians
and other public figures who, at a time of growing witch hunts, did not
wish to appear soft on traitors. It was egged on by a public still much
under the influence of traditional racial prejudices and far from free of
the anti-Japanese hatreds of the recent war."

In the midst of all the hullabaloo, Iva's troubles continued to mount.
She entered a hospital to give birth to a baby boy, who died a half-day
later.

That blow devastated Iva Toguri. In addition, she came down with a
severe inflammation of the joints and was bedridden for some time.

At first the jury in her trial reported to the judge that they were
hopelessly deadlocked. (The first ballot had been ten to two in Toguri's
favor.) At this point most judges would have declared a mistrial, but
Judge Roche urged the jury to renew their deliberations. (This judge
was reported later to be strongly prejudiced against Iva, having said pri-
vately he believed her to be guilty, even before the verdict.)

This time the jury returned a verdict of guilty on only one of the
eight counts: she had made a broadcast in which she said, "Orphans
of the Pacific, you are really orphans now. How will you get home
now that your ships are sunk?" This was just after the splendid
American naval victory at the Battle of Leyte Gulf.

In charging the jury Judge Roche had instructed them that in order
to convict Iva Toguri of the charge of treason, they would have to find,
first of all, that she had been a U.S. citizen at the time of the alleged
overt act or acts. Everyone seemed to be agreed that she was. The
defense had pointed out that Iva had refused to renounce her American
citizenship or take advantage of her marriage to Filipe d'Aquino to
enter the haven of Portuguese nationality.

Next, the judge said, it would have to be shown that Iva had had the
intent to harm her country by giving "aid and comfort" to its enemy.
(By this definition the amoral gadfly Jane Fonda would deserve the
charge of being a traitor much more than Iva Toguri.)

Nor would intent alone be sufficient, even if it could be proved, Roche went on. It would have to be supported by a provable overt act to realize that intent.

To back up this allegation, there were no radio scripts in which Iva Toguri was shown to utter the above message, "Orphans of the Pacific." Nor were there any recordings of such a broadcast with her voice clearly identifiable.

Two witnesses brought from Japan had testified they heard Iva make the crucial broadcast. Both were American Nisei who had been threatened that they themselves might be charged with treason if they did not testify for the prosecution at Iva's trial. (Both had been employed at Radio Tokyo and could have heard such a broadcast, if one had been made, or read such a script.)

Whether or not Iva actually uttered those words is moot. The "proof" that she did is flimsy. If she did say those words, which Iva stated she did not remember saying, they could be interpreted as an attempt to give "aid and comfort" to the enemy.

From this point of view, Iva Toguri was probably guilty of treason according to Judge Roche's definition and deserved some form of punishment (although nothing nearly so draconian as the sentence she got—ten years in prison.)

The ever-eloquent Edwin O. Reischauer summed it all up very neatly: "The whole story is sad and often sordid. (Iva) herself was naive and foolish. Harassment, intimidation, distortion of truth, even falsification of evidence by so-called law enforcement officers proved all too common. There was clear judicial bias and a press seeking sensationalism rather than truth."

Reischauer continued, "It is sad to note that Iva Toguri was harassed and then jailed for years as the mythical 'Tokyo Rose' because she was so American. She steadfastly refused to do the easy thing in wartime Japan and accept Japanese citizenship. She remained confident of final American victory and of American justice. She refused to abandon the United States, though her country, by playing false to its own ideals of justice, certainly abandoned her."

A strange case, indeed.

## References

1.  Duus, Masayo. *Tokyo Rose, Orphan of the Pacific.* Tokyo: Kodansha International, 1979.

2.  "Tokyo Rose." *San Francisco Sunday Examiner and Chronicle*, November 14, 1971.

3.  Krasano, Rena. *Strangers Always.* Berkeley, California: Pacific View Press, 1992.

4.  Gayn, Mark. *Japan Diary.* New York: William Sloane, 1948.

5.  Howe, Russell W. *The Hunt for Tokyo Rose.* Lanham, Md.: Madison Books, 1993.

## CHAPTER TEN

# Xmas Paint Your Harts

*Being in Japan in those days was better than going to a vaudeville show. It was a laugh a minute. One American half-seriously wondered if they had a new strategy—to defeat us with laughter. If so, they nearly succeeded.*

### TOKYO 1945—AND BEYOND

During the Christmas season, the first after the Pacific war, I was out in the warm winter sunshine enjoying a Sunday amble down the Ginza, the main commercial street in central Tokyo. Christmas meant little in Japan, especially in those desperate times, so the pedestrians were mostly fellow Americans; the Japanese had little time or money for shopping in the street's forlorn-looking emporiums.

As I approached the Matsuzakaya Department Store, I saw a mammoth vertical banner hanging from the fifth to the first floor of the building. Four black English words were boldly inscribed on the white cloth:

### XMAS PAINT YOUR HARTS

Other GIs had also stopped to gaze at the department store's message. I overheard one of them say to another, "Now what the devil do you suppose that means?"

Being unable to enlighten him, I walked on, lost in the wonder of it. Although I did not know it then, this was the first of a long, long series of my encounters in Japan with the strange world of Fractured English (also called Japlish or Translation Sensations.)

The many other examples of this peculiar variety of English that I encountered over the following years were often delightful, hilarious, or just plain weird, but they were instructive in that they showed us a people striving mightily to communicate with a horde of foreigners dropped suddenly in their midst, efforts that even when laughable at least deserved top grades for effort. (After all, few of us could ask the time of day in Japanese.) And with the passage of time I found that some of these instances of broken English had a piquant charm that somehow communicated the speaker's meaning even better than correct English might have.

An example of this latter variety was a sign in front of the Nikko Botanical Gardens that read, "No Botanizing, drinking, or up roaring, etc. in the garden." That left no doubt about what they meant and made a lasting impression.

The language of signs (or "Sign Langwich," as one Japanese sign-painter advertised his product) offered a most fruitful field, with little gems like these:

"Fondle dogs" (from a pet shop in Osaka).

"We wash you" (from a carwash in Kawasaki).

"Guaranteed Pure Gold Fish" (from a goldfish peddler's cart).

"Specialist for the Decease of Children" (From an Osaka pediatrician's office).

"Extract of fowl" (from a store that sold eggs).

ONE SIGN at the airport in Haneda seemed uncannily to predict the future of airline baggage services all over the world: "We Take Your Bags and Send Them in All Directions."

Hotels were also fertile hunting grounds for the happy Fractured English hunter:

"Use this elevator. Fright Elevator in repair." (In the Shiba Hotel in Tokyo).

"The elevator is fixed for the next day. During that time we regret you will be unbearable." (In a Niigata hostelry).

"Our hotel serves ten in a bag — like Mother." (In an inn near the docks in Kobe).

"Rooms are changing their boys and girls." (Notice left in each room in an American engineers' billet in Yokohama, presumably by the room-boy).

"Room-boy is a present." (From a card attached to a small gift left in the author's room in Tokyo's Dai Ichi Hotel).

Example of fractured English.

ALTHOUGH I never found proof of my suspicions, I used to imagine that somewhere down in the dark cellars under the national police force's headquarters in Tokyo, there dwelt a gnarled gnome of a man with unkempt hair and a fanatic glint in his eyes. Ensconced among his trusty lexicons, he was charged with the English translation of all the traffic signs that were to be erected along the roads and streets of his country.

It was his little empire ("Mine! All Mine!") and his translations were never to be questioned. His word was god-like and final and he never deigned to check his translations with native speakers of English for accuracy. Among his masterpieces were:

"Cars will not have intercourse on this bridge." (From a bridge near Fukuoka).

"Let's Reduce Noise by Ourselves." (In one particular year, there were hundreds of these signs erected all along the byways of Japan).

"Vertical parking only." (A sign on the street in front of the old Teito Hotel in Tokyo).

"Quietly!" (This sign was also erected by the hundreds or even thousands throughout the country. The Japanese equivalent was "*Shizuka ni,*" which can, of course, be rendered as "Quietly!" but which in this instance carries with it the strong connotation of "Be calm, slow down, take care.")

"Have many accidents here!" (A sign at the Roppongi intersection in Tokyo).

The last of the above nearly caused an international incident when the author first sighted it. It must have been the devil that made me do it, but I sped to a near-by police station and explained that, being a law-abiding and thoroughly decent sort of fellow, I insisted on obeying traffic signs to their precise letter and therefore wanted to know just where I should have the accidents referred to on the sign and how many persons I should endeavor to have injured in them. A surly lot, the Roppongi police could see little if any humor in this and made certain threats against my person that were not at all warranted.

Akin to the traffic-sign gnome in the police cellar, there was also, I was confident, an absolute linguistic genius squirreled away backstage in that marvelous hall of pleasure: the Nichigeki Theater. He was the man who, for many years, made up the titles—all in flawless(?) English—for the song and dance productions presented in the Nichigeki Music Hall on the fourth floor. It greatly behooves some ardent young researcher to go through the Nichigeki ads in old newspaper files and record for future enlightenment the magnificent titles that this genius concocted. I remember only three, but they were jim dandies:

"Titillate Me Purple in the Tulip Time".

"Shag and Shimmy at the Shine-town Shindig".

"Three Dervishes at a Whippenpoof Whingding".

JUST ACROSS the alley from the Nichigeki stood the Asahi Building, where labored the editors of the *Asahi Evening News*. One of these fellows dreamed up the idea of a contest in which his English-language newspaper would offer ¥1,000 for examples of weird, Japanized English. This contest produced some spanking good ones, including, I recall, a photograph of a medicine bottle, the label of which read: "Adults: Take three tablets a day until passing away." Finally, however, the great, gray eminence of the *Asahi* got caught on its own toils the day they ran this headline: "Solution to Laotian Crisis Remains Unsolved."

Lest I be accused of poking fun only at the Japanese, I hasten to point out that during those same years we Westerners in Japan must have been guilty of monumental bloopers in Japanese that had even the reserved and polite Japanese rolling in the aisles.

Sadly, one has to understand the Japanese tongue to appreciate these offenses against correct speech, but I can give a hint of their grossness by pointing out two Japanese words similar in spelling but quite different in meaning. *Komon* means advisor, but *koomon* means anal exit, the only difference being the long or short sound of the first 'o' in the two words.

The author had an American acquaintance who once introduced himself at a conference of Japanese businessmen with the Japanese equivalent of the sentence "I am Mr. Sasakawa's advisor." At least, that is what he intended to say—but he inadvertently used the long 'o' instead of the short 'o', and in doing so, broke up the conference.

In a window sign, a department store in Niigata preened itself about one of its items of merchandise: "Our nylons cost more than common but will find best for long run."

In general, not only department stores but also tailors, dressmakers, and fashion shops were quite lavish with their Fractured English creations:

"New and Old Clothes Fix Civilized Style." (From a Nihombashi tailor shop).

"We Make Fur Out of Your Skin." (From a fashionable fur shop on the Namiki-dori in Tokyo).

"Stateside Stile" (from a Ueno dressmaker's store).

"Ladies Have Fits Upstairs" (that old classic from a dressmaker's establishment near the Daibutsu statue in Kamakura).

"Dresses for Ladies and Gentlemen" (chiseled in the marble façade above a Ginza clothing store).

"European Monkey Jacket Make for Japanese" (example quoted in a book by B.H. Chamberlain).

"Unthinkable color combinations" (Ladies sportswear store in Shinjuku).

Many jewels were mined in bars (where we found "Old American Whiskey—Established 1492" and "Old Airship Whisky—Since Early 1800's") and in restaurants' menus, such as:

| | |
|---|---|
| "Sardine Sand" | "Humbug Steak" |
| "Cuban Livers" | "Rogue Fart Cheese" |
| "Beef Strong Nuff" | "Prown and Poison Au Gratin" |

One Shinjuku bar yielded in its toilet the carefully-lettered sign: "To stop drip, turn cock to right."

Other unforgettable examples:

An ad in the Asahi newspaper was entirely in Japanese except its five-word headline: "Smooth as a baby's ass."

A commercial establishment outside Camp Zama announced its new business activity: "No more whorehouse. Now Number One laundry. You come all same, please."

A sign in front of the Shimokitazawa Station: "Don't urine water."

In the brochure of a tour bus company: "Tour the backside of Japan."

A sign in the window of a bakery in Kanda: "Today (Jan. 1) is holiday. After Jan. 4, we begin giving you the Business."

The widely publicized motto of the Japan Toilet Society: "Clean, Fresh, I am Toilet."

The back of a teenager's sweatshirt: "Many things un-understandable, a chicken-hearted seems slim usually."

Another sweatshirt read: "Mr. Zog's original sex wax. Never spoils. It's best for your stick."

A barber's invitation: "Heads cutting ¥1,500. For bald men ¥900."

The famous Deer Park in Nara warned its visitors to "Beware of Bucks with Long Horns." (Take your time, ladies. Don't push. The train for Nara doesn't leave for another hour.)

On the window of a photographer's studio was painted "Photo- grapher Executed," and in the same neighborhood stood a sundries store with the sign, "Sun Light Soap—Lever Brothels, Ltd."

For a while I puzzled over an English-language map of Tokyo, showing a location near Tokyo Bay with the description, "Dirty Water Punishment Place." Checking the original Japanese, I learned it was a Sewage Disposal Plant, but the linguistic complications leading from there to "Dirty Water Punishment Place" are too lengthy and tortuous to set down here.

Another strange sign was found in a suburban Tokyo shop window with no other indication as to the nature of the store or what product or service it wanted to sell. I never did enter the store to find out; I think I was uneasy about what I might be told. The sign in its entirety, read: "Come in and have your thing engraved."

Aside from the levity, there were, of course, more serious facets to the Japanese inability to transmit somber, even potentially fatal, messages in English. In *Japan's Imperial Conspiracy*, author David Bergamini tells of a poster he saw in a Japanese internee encampment in the Philippines:

*Still the Igorot peoples living in and about Baguio continue to put the fire on or to loot something from the properties in and about Baguio. This is not good behavior anyway. When the Imperial Japanese Army finds out those who intend to do so, it will shoot them by guns.*

*Signed*
*Affectionately yours,*
*Lt. Col. Kanmori*
*Imperial Japanese Army*

In *Things Japanese* B.H. Chamberlain mentioned a booklet distributed to Japanese policemen entitled, *The Practical Use of (English) Conversation for Police Authorities*, which is divided into such chapters as "Cordinal Number," "Official Tittle," and "Ports of the Body."

Under "Misseranious Subjects" is offered an imagined conversation between a Japanese policeman and a British sailor:

| | |
|---|---|
| Policeman: | "What countryman are you?" |
| Sailor: | "I am sailor belonged to the *Golden Eagle*, the British man-of-war." |
| Policeman: | "Why do you strike this *jinrikisha* man?" |
| Sailor: | "He told me impolitely." |
| Policeman: | "What does he told you impolitely?" |
| Sailor: | "He insulted me saying loudly 'the Sailor, the Sailor' when I am passing here." |
| Policeman: | "Do you striking this man for that?" |
| Sailor: | "Yes." |
| Policeman: | "But do not strike him for it is forbidded." |
| Sailor: | "Okey-dokey. I strike him no more." |

Toward the end of this booklet, the author himself appears to have his own private doubts about what he was wrought, for he injects a conversation between two policemen that ends on this note:

| | |
|---|---|
| First policeman: | "You speak English very well." |
| Second policeman: | "You jest." |

Not so far back in time these traffic instructions were distributed by a police station in Osaka:

1. At the rise of hand policeman, stop rapidly. do not pass him by or otherwise disrespect him.

2. When a passenger of the foot have in view, tottle the horn; trumpet at him melodiously at first, but if he still obstacles your passage, tootle him with vigor and express by word of mouth warning "Hi, Hi."

3.  Beware of the wandering horse, cow or pig that they shall not take fright as you pass them by. Do not explode the exhaust box at them. Go soothingly by.

4.  Give great space to the festive dog that shall sport in the roadway.

5.  Avoid entanglement of dog with wheel spokes.

6.  Go soothingly on the grease road as there lurks the skid demon.

7.  Press the brake of the foot as you roll around corner to save collapse and tie-up.

Douglas MacArthur's Japanese supporters erected this banner.

*Drawing by J. R. Britt, Magnolia, Texas*

Quite possibly the one classic instance of Fractured English in Japan that must tower head, shoulders, and torso over all competition was seen when Douglas MacArthur was still enthroned in Tokyo and being promoted as a possible candidate in the pending U.S. presidential election. A group of ardent Japanese supporters of the already aging American general arranged to have a gigantic banner hoisted high over the busy Hibiya intersection in downtown Tokyo, just where

MacArthur could see it when he emerged from his office in the Dai Ichi Building. Bearing in mind that the Japanese tend to confuse the R and the L in English, try to visualize these six-foot high letters that were emblazoned on the banner "We Pray for MacArthur's Erection"

### References

1.  *Tokyo Weekender.* Tokyo: December 17, 1982.

2.  Chamberlain, Basil Hall. *Things Japanese.* London: John Murray, 1905.

A Ginza department store sends holiday greetings to one and all during the first postwar Christmas. *Drawing by J. R. Britt, Magnolia, Texas*

## CHAPTER ELEVEN

# *Manga:* The Literature of the Nation?

*Westerners tend to think of the Japanese as a serious, hard-working, eager-beaver race who forever have their noses in manuals and books of science. A glimpse into the comics business may suggest other inclinations.*

JAPAN, THE PRESENT DAY

The most popular comic book in the United States, Marvel Comics' *X-Men*, racks up annual sales of about five million. Compare that to *Shonen Jump* in Japan which reports two hundred million—forty times as many, with only about half the population.

Strange to relate, the Japanese comics industry is one with many such eye-opening statistics. In 1995 two-and-a-quarter- billion comic magazines and books were sold and that figure is increasing yearly. By number of volumes this amounted to 40 percent of all books and magazines purchased. In monetary terms, the figure was less—23 percent—but on the other hand the rate of unsold returns (from bookstore to publisher) was much higher for the non-comics.

Japan is the world's largest consumer of comics. Seventy percent of high school students read comics regularly, while the comparable figure in the United States is only fifteen percent.

Critics have styled these comics—the *manga*—Japan's "postwar literature." Many believe they exert more influence on the populace than either newspapers or television. Five hundred categories of *manga* flood into the bookstores, newsstands, and vending machines each month and cover the entire range of human activity. They are both an entertainment medium and an educational tool.

In 1986 a 1,000-page guidebook to the Japanese economy in cartoon form (*Nihon Keizai Nyumon*) achieved a record-breaking $15 million in sales in Japan alone. Published in the United States as *Japan Inc., A Comic*, it has been used as a text in several universities.

The Japanese government has published some of its white papers in the form of comic books while the Ministry of International Trade and Industry distributes comic books about foreign aid. (The latter would be most appropriate in this country, considering the way we Americans conduct that charitable enterprise.)

Back in 1983 the rise and fall in the prices of certain stocks struck some observers as bizarre, leading to studies that found the buying and selling of those stocks followed the advice given in a biweekly comic strip called *Manju Kowai* (Bean Cakes Are Scary).

THE WORD *manga* literally means "whimsical sketches" and was coined early in the nineteenth century by woodblock artist Hokusai. Now it covers everything from animated films to political cartoons in newspapers, but the word most often brings to mind comic books filled with minimal dialogue (but much onomatopoeia), action-packed illustrations, faces characterized by expressive eyes and contorted features, and graphic scenes of frantic, uninhibited sexual activity (at least in the so-called adult comics).

The prevailing influence of comics in Japan is explained by Dr. Masahiko Ito, who has psychoanalyzed some of the *manga* characters: "While people laugh at the *manga*, they are unconsciously learning how to behave and what not to do. Everyone is controlled from a young age, so the fantasies (in the *manga*) are extremely important."

It is necessary, agree many others, in a repressed society like Japan's to provide safety valves. The *enka*—the maudlin folk songs men sing in karaoke bars—is one of them. Falling-down drunkenness is another. The *bonen-kai* ("forget-the-old-year-parties")—at which an employee can get just about anything off his chest to his boss—is a third. And then there are the escape fantasies of the comics.

Standing tall among the *manga* are the *ero-manga*, or erotic comics. These have their progenitors in the lecherous woodblock prints produced in immense quantities in the eighteenth and nineteenth centuries—and have followed a rocky road since.

There are times when the police, who serve as censors, are content to advise the *ero-manga* publishers to practice "self-restraint" and then leave them pretty much up to their own devices. At other times, under pressure from segments of the public, they increase their surveillance and even demand the withdrawal of certain extremely raunchy editions from the market, which can bankrupt a smaller publisher.

Not long ago the gendarmes arrested a man for the murder of several young girls. When his apartment was searched, a mountain of *ero-manga* and erotic video tapes was uncovered.

Packs of infuriated women, with Parent Teacher Associations baying in the vanguard, claimed to have discovered a direct trail from the *ero-manga* to crimes involving the abuse and murder of children. In full voice, they clamorously demanded that the police put a stop to the Lolita mania by mangling the *ero-manga* publishers and next dismembering the writers and artists of these excursions into erotica.

Responding, the police cracked down, first calling for *jiyu-kisei*, or self-regulation. Hard-porn became soft-porn and for a short while all was comparatively well. But to expect total and effective censorship of the *ero-manga* by the police would be condemning them to the labor of Sisyphus. There are several regulations governing the sale of *ero-manga*, and one of them is that if more than one-third of a magazine contains scenes of naked bodies or bodies in "sexual positions," it must not be sold to children. Quite reasonable.

But the problem is that a bookstore may receive one or two dozen different *ero-manga* every morning and the proprietor will not—indeed, cannot—take the time to go through each one and calculate the percentage of offending pages. Nor, in fact, would the police, should they make a spot inspection.

Then there is Article 175 of the Criminal Code which makes it illegal to graphically depict adult genitalia, pubic hair, and sexual intercourse. The operative word in the first phrase of this prohibition is "adult."

Many non-erotic comics targeted at girls between eleven and thirteen often feature nudity, including occasional glimpses of the privates. The Japanese, it seems, have never been overly concerned about the depiction of nakedness or incipient sexual curiosity in children. Perhaps this is because any such activities on the part of persons under, say, eleven or twelve years of age do not seriously blemish a family's good name or undermine its stability. And, of course, it is the family or group, not the individual, that is more important in Japan.

In fact, there is a body of opinion in Japan, sometimes expressed even by the usually anti-*ero-manga* PTAs, that holds that if children did not have access to these sexual fantasies in print, they might indulge in real-life sexual experiments, which could be worse.

This studied indifference to nudity and suggestions of sexual arousal in children has presented a window of opportunity for *ero-manga* of the *Rori-kon* genre, *Rori* deriving from Lolita and *kon* from complex. In extreme but not necessarily infrequent instances, these magazines show adults enjoying sexual adventures with little girls—perhaps because grown women could not be graphically depicted instead.

These particular *ero-manga* often announce their nature through their names: *Loli-Touch, Loli-Pop, Loli-Party*, inter alia. They are a far cry from what would be acceptable today in the United States, where V. Nabokov published the novel that named the complex. Other *ero-manga*, of which there are at least one hundred, go by such appellations as *Lewd Labia Diary, Lemon Angel, Make Me Feel Baby, No-Panty Angels, It's Time to Have Adventures, Pink Parsley*, and *Hot Pants*.

To further mesmerize the *ero-manga* maniacs, one artifice of the Lolita-mania artists is to make their girls look even younger than they are in reality. The narration may subtly indicate that the actual age of the female youngster depicted is seventeen or eighteen, but she may be drawn with short curls and shorter skirts (and appear to Western eyes to be only ten or so).

What is the appeal of these young girls to devotees of the *Rori-kon ero-manga*? Is it that the girls are seen as easier to manipulate in male fantasies? Or, because they are virginal but sexually curious, they incite in the male reader an urge to be the first to introduce them to the joys of sex—to be remembered fondly by her for that reason ever after?

And, to be sure, very young girls usually do not have any pubic hair, the slightest depiction of which might bring the paddy wagon with siren wailing. For it is the sight of *chimo* (shameful hair) with which the Japanese appear to have a somewhat inexplicable hang-up.

A well-known instance of this comose concern was an American magazine, *Playboy*, that carried color photos of naked women whose pubic hair could be seen. Horrified, the Japanese authorities quickly forbade the importation of *Playboy*, so the importer employed part-time Pubic Hair Expurgators—mostly housewives and college students—to carefully obliterate (with air brushes) all such hair in every copy of the periodical. (At one time, the number imported monthly was 25,000).

In today's domestic *ero-manga*, the proscription is sometimes ignored—as is that against the delineation of genitalia—especially since the changes of 1993. Even so, to be on the safe side, the writer/artists resort to symbolism. They draw substitutes. Instead of a lingam* shape, they ink in eggplants, cucumbers, the heads of turtles, snakes, and even steam locomotives. In place of a yoni,† they will offer the reader conch shells, tunnels, and assorted mollusks.

In the March 1995 issue of *Kansai Time Out*, Mr. Mizuno of the Child Protection Section of the Osaka prefectural government was interviewed and stated that there are two different perceptions of child pornography. One—which Mr. Mizuno rejects—is that the *ero-manga* exert much influence on how youngsters feel about sexual activity. The second—which he supports—is that no study (known to him) shows a direct link between the *ero-manga* and improper sexual behavior on the part of children.

* the phallic symbol under which Siva is worshipped.
† a representation of the female genitals, under which Shakti is worshipped.

The regulations of his department in Osaka are stricter than those of most other prefectures in Japan, so he cannot justify even tougher suppression of access to the *ero-manga* by children. And it must be admitted that this massive outpouring of sexual fact and fantasy seemingly has not spawned a depraved horde of panting, promiscuous youngsters. At least, not yet.

Other less specific uses of symbols may require some understanding of Japanese culture in order to follow. For instance, sexual excitement in a man may be signified by blood gushing from his nose. Or, should he become lost in lascivious fancies, the distance between his upper lip and his nose elongates. And, of course, there are always the old international standbys of gathering storm clouds, sweaty faces, clenched fists, and pounding surfs.

The first *ero-manga* to catch my attention (I remember it well even today) was about a male school teacher who had undertaken to teach two little neighborhood girls—ages eight and eleven—all about sex, and he went about this in a competently professorial manner. In the midst of these high-jinks, the mother of the busy girls chanced upon the scene and exclaimed, "My goodness, teach, what is it that you are doing there?"

The teacher, who maintains a cool demeanor throughout, replies, "Nothing much. Just a continuation of the educational process." Apparently reassured, the mother watches with keen interest until this grade-school docent fastens his academic gaze on her. Before you know it, they whisper a few salacious nothings to each other and head for home, with the little girls in tow.

The last scene shows the teacher and the mother entangled in Position 34 of the Standard 48 Japanese Positions while the little girls—both naked as peeled apples—stand watchfully beside them and make admiring comments on the teacher's style.

Before that, even the act of kissing was almost never seen in girls' comics, but today's *ero-manga* for either sex show abortion, incest, and homosexuality with frequency and fervor. (The first time a couple was shown kissing in a postwar movie, the actress is said to have had a strip of cellophane covering her lips. And earlier, in the late nineteenth century, the Japanese—whose men and women often bathed together unabashed in communal bath houses—were scandalized by Western oil paintings of single naked women.)

Once it was widely believed that the *ero-manga* were devoted mostly to scenes of men happily abusing women. I have in my collection an issue of *Champion* magazine, which carries a finely drawn depiction of a naked woman hanging by her wrists which are tied to a beam in a barn, while a man—her husband— pours a bucket of bovine urine over her. "That'll teach you not to serve me cold rice," he is saying. This predisposition to show the woman who is boss has not, regrettably, faded out completely, but it is clearly waning and in fact antipodal scenes are to be found increasingly.

It is reported that the majority of *ero-manga* readers are men, but who is to say how many females blushingly peruse those comics furtively (?) fetched home by male relatives. It is entirely possible that the *ero-manga* of today serve in the role played by the *makura-e* of the Edo era (1603–1867).

IN THOSE bygone days, doting parents placed *makura-e* under their soon-to-wed daughters' pillows. These so-called "pillow pictures" were actually illustrated sex manuals showing the bride-to-be everything that might be done to her or that she might be expected to do to her bridegroom on their wedding night.

Although the girls of today cannot expect to be so lucky as to find that a Japanese Tooth Fairy has deposited a how-to book about sex under their pillows, they may well be able to fulfill their need-to-know by peeking under their brother's bed or into their father's briefcase.

Many *ero-manga* are undeniably crude, sadistic, and offensively depraved—but not all of them. Not by any means. Many are well drawn, sometimes refined and subtle, and occasionally quite humorous. (Recently, while reading one marvelous series by a writer/artist with the pen name of Hikaru Yuzuki, I fell off my chair choking on laughter. My wife had to be physically dissuaded from summoning emergency medical services.)


## References

1.  Schodt, Frederick L. *Manga! Manga! The World of Japanese Comics*. New York: Kodansha, 1983.

2.  Seward, Jack. *Japanese Eroticism*. Houston: Yugen Press, 1993.

3.  Scott, Paul. "Pornography." *Kansai Time Out* (Osaka), S.U. Press, March 1995.

4.  Perton, Marc. "How Japanese-style Comics Are Taking Over the World." *Business Tokyo*, February 1991.

5.  "Comics Serious Business in Japan." *Houston Post*, September 20, 1987.

6.  "Japan's Comics Serious Business." *Houston Post*, February 9, 1996.

7.  Seward, Jack. *More About the Japanese*. Tokyo: Lotus Press, 1983.

## CHAPTER TWELVE

# The Reincarnation of Jesus Christ in Japan?

◄━━━━►

*It was believed that this handsome youth could run (not walk) on water and summon birds to lay eggs in his hand. Was he the Messiah? Many Japanese Christians believed he was. At Shimabara, 37,000 of them died at his side to demonstrate that belief.*

### SOUTHWESTERN JAPAN 1637

Jesus Christ did not specify where on this earth he would make his Second Coming, but we have no good reason to believe he might not land in Japan as well as in any other country. Nor do we know just what the savior looked like since no portraits were made of him while he was living. When he descends once more to earth, Christ could have the face and form of a Japanese or an Australian or a Zulu.

Might he deign to come among us for the second time as a young boy with the face of an angel? A Christian who worked miracles and who was the spiritual leader of his people? Who, at the unseasoned age of sixteen, was the commander-in-chief of an army of 40,000 and who was willing to—indeed, did—die for his religion?

Many called this wonderful lad the Messiah and he trod his stage in the 1630s on Japan's southern island of Kyushu. His true name was Shiro Masuda but throughout the last five years of his life he was called Shiro Amakusa. Amakusa (Heavenly Grass) is the name of the

archipelago off the western shore of Kyushu—islands of such heavenly beauty one cannot gaze upon them for long without water forming
in the eyes. Shiro came from one of those cone-like islets where
Christianity far outnumbered all other religions.

IN 1549, three Jesuit missionaries landed in Kagoshima at the southern
tip of Japan. To these Catholic priests, one of whom was St. Francis
Xavier, must go the credit for bringing Christianity to Japan.

Statue of Shiro Amakusa, the Japanese Messiah.
*Courtesy of Minami Arima-machi City Office, Education Committee*

Between that year and 1635, these and other missionaries who followed
did what was, on the surface at least, a truly remarkable job of converting the Japanese to Christianity. In 1582, there were eighty missionaries and 150,000 converts in Japan, but, by 1635, the year of the ultimate

repression, the number of converts had grown to somewhere between 200,000 and 300,000 and included many *daimyo*, generals, and persons of cultural and material attainments.

Several factors, however, must be considered in connection with these reported conversions. First, certain similarities (candles, images, rosaries, altar flowers, incense, processions, and the shaven heads of priests) between Catholicism and Buddhism led many Japanese to believe that the newly imported religion was still another of the numerous sects of Buddhism and, as such, had the approval of one thousand years of custom and familiarity.

Second, the Japanese were quick to note that merchants with exotic commodities and firearms often accompanied the priests, so the many desiring to trade assumed that a warm welcome given the religious half of the team would result in reciprocity from the commercial half.

Third, the priests devoted their staunchest efforts at proselytization to the feudal lords, who, if won over, sometimes ordered their subjects to become Christians en masse (and who were also known, when disappointed with the resultant material and spiritual benefits, to abruptly command their people to revert to Buddhism with equal ease).

Fourth, the missionaries had given medical care to many among the lower class converts.

Fifth, often the Japanese were favorably impressed mostly by the erudition of the priests and struck by their unusual appearance.

Last, the Christian timing was apt, for the powerful Nobunaga Oda (1543–1582) was bent on unifying the country and welcomed the Christians as a weapon for use against the unruly Buddhist monasteries in and around Kyoto.

Although Nobunaga's successor Hideyoshi Toyotomi was at first tolerant of the Christians and their activities, his benignity turned to dark distrust when he was told by Protestant traders from England and Holland that the Catholic missionaries were harbingers of Spanish soldiery, who would, as in the case of Mexico and the Philippines, conquer while the priests converted.

In 1587, Hideyoshi issued an edict banning Christianity but did not begin to enforce it until ten years later, when he had nine Catholic missionaries and seventeen Japanese converts crucified. (The Japanese courage and equanimity in the face of this difficult death is said to have exceeded that of their foreign mentors—the first time that Catholicism had encountered such fortitude in non-Europeans.)

Hideyoshi died before he could carry out his intent to obliterate Christianity. His successor Ieyasu Tokugawa was at first too beguiled by the potential of trade with Europe to take up the cudgels himself against the men of God. At length, however, he too became distrustful and then outright antagonistic and so initiated a series of repressive measures that culminated in the massacre of thirty-seven thousand Christian converts in Shimabara in early 1638. Some authorities believe the Shimabara Rebellion drew as much momentum from economic and political unrest as from religious differences; it just happened to take place in a district in which many Christians lived. Nevertheless, the rebellion brought on the expulsion of the missionaries, an absolute interdiction against all Christian converts and activity, and the closure of Japan's gates to the world (except for a handful of non-Catholic European traders on the island of Dejima in Nagasaki harbor) for more than two hundred years.

Christianity in Japan has never fully recovered from this Tokugawa hostility and suppression. There were, to be sure, brief subsequent periods of enthusiastic interest, so much so that in the 1880s one leading magistrate went so far as to predict that Christianity might well become Japan's official state religion.

The pendulum swung back and forth. The news of *soi-disant* peace-loving Christian nations slaughtering each other in the bloody trenches of World War I gave would-be converts in Japan food for thought, counterbalanced by the humanitarianism of Woodrow Wilson's idealistic Fourteen Points and the unstinting aid sent to Japan after the Great Kanto Earthquake of 1923. Then, in 1924, the U.S. Congress passed the Oriental Exclusion Act, probably doing the American reputation more injury than anything else could have, short of out-and-out war.

Since 1872, when the government lifted its ban on Christianity, all missionaries have been free to proselytize in Japan and doubtless they must be credited with having done many good works. Even so,

Christianity is not a major influence today: less than one percent of the Japanese are even nominally converted and many Japanese will tell you they attended Sunday school (and church) as youngsters only to get the candy the preachers and priests passed out.

Although the motives of many of the Japanese who embraced Christianity during the years between 1549 and 1638 may be questioned, there can be little doubt that at least some of them had faith of the highest and firmest order, for within a month after the construction of a Roman Catholic church in Nagasaki in 1865, four thousand Japanese Christians from the nearby village of Urakami came to the church to rejoice and to explain to the priest that they and their forebears had secretly kept the Christian faith alive for 230 years. Although Japan was then in the process of opening its doors to the West, the laws against Christianity were still in force, and the Tokugawa Shogunate arrested all four thousand and banished them to isolated islands. Fortunately, the Tokugawa regime collapsed before more serious harm could befall this stout-hearted assemblage. Ironically, this same Catholic church, which the four thousand faithful from Urakami later joined, met complete destruction at American hands when the second atomic bomb was dropped on Nagasaki in August 1945.

NOW COMES marching into the early Tokugawa era one Shiro (his Christian name was Jerome) Amakusa, whose favorite white banner carried the brave device that when translated from the Portuguese read, "Praised be the Holiest of Sacraments!"

Twenty-five years earlier a poem written by a Jesuit priest contained the lines:

*This boy, possessing since birth every gift,*
*Without effort will demonstrate his marvelous power*
*Then Heaven will make the clouds flame in the east and west*
*And earth will cause the flowers to bloom before their Time.*

The Christians in Kyushu knew this verse and waited to see if its prophecy would come true. Sure enough, in the year Shiro's rebellion

began, an odd red glow was observed at dawn and in the early dusk—
and cherry blossoms bloomed in autumn, not in the spring.

Other stories spread of Shiro's miraculous powers. He could, it was
said, summon birds on wing to alight on his hand, and if he was of a
mind, make them lay eggs there. He could run across the surface of the
sea and once he splashed past a flaming crucifix that had risen out of the
waves. With this ammunition, the Christians went one step further and
boldly proclaimed Shiro Amakusa, when he was still only fifteen, to be
the reincarnation of Jesus Christ.

In the Christian districts of Shimabara and the Amakusa islands
(almost within sight off to the southwest) the pauperized peasants
prayed for succor from their desperate circumstances. Harvests were
scant in Kyushu after 1634 with a monumental crop failure in 1637.
The farmers had been reduced, literally, to eating mud and straw.

In lieu of alleviating taxes, the several *daimyo* of western Kyushu
seemed to liken the farmers to sesame seeds, of which it was said, "The
harder you squeeze them, the more (oil) they give."

In addition to these economic agonies, the government had begun to
enforce the anti-Christian edicts already on its books. As a test to ascer-
tain a person's religious inclinations, he was directed to step on a *fumi-
e* (literally, a trod-on picture) which was an image of Jesus Christ carved
on a metal plaque and sunk in a floor. Anyone willing to defile this
image by stepping on it as presumed not to be a Christian.

This was but the beginning. With the Christians still making no
effort at concerted resistance, more forms of torture were put to use:
face-branding, the snake pit, roasting alive, crucifixion, and amputation
of limbs with bamboo saws.

Peasants who refused to renounce Christianity were lowered into
the extremely hot waters of the Unzen Hot Springs and allowed to
slowly boil to death. At the other extreme a pregnant wife in Amakusa
was put into a "cold water vat" for seven days and allowed to die of
exposure—but not until she had given birth to her infant underwater.

One *daimyo*, Lord Matsukura, devised a devilish kind of excrucia-
tion called the *mino-odori*, *mino* being a farmer's straw raincoat and
*odori* meaning dance. The fiendish idea was to truss the victim up in

this straw raincoat, drench the coat in lamp oil, and set it ablaze. The tormented writhings and contortions of the soon-to-die rustic were thought to resemble an awkward, if pathetic dance.

Lord Matsukura delighted in having these acrobatics performed just after dusk, when they would give the illusion of fireworks for his assembled guests.

This religious abuse was accompanied by levies that grew ever more extortionate: the rice tax, hearth tax, door tax, cattle tax, shelf tax, and taxes on each death and birth in a family.

In December 1637, the young, comely daughter of a village headman was taken into custody and hanged upside down, naked. Her tormentors branded her entire body with irons that were glowing hot. No place on her body was without its angry red welt. Her father had thought that his child would merely be imprisoned until he paid his debt in taxes, but when he learned of her death by branding, he became insane with grief and killed the bailiff responsible. The death of the bailiff convinced the neighbors that the entire community might well be annihilated as punishment, and they determined to no longer meekly accept their chastisement.

One foreign observer, Pages, believed this incident was the igniter in the tinderbox. The *Shimabara no ran* (Shimabara Rebellion) burst into wildfire on December 17, 1637, and spread through the Shimabara Peninsula and across to the Amakusa islands.

Quickly, young Shiro Amakusa was chosen as the rebel leader. He was believed to have performed miracles. He was an eloquent preacher. He was handsome—with the beautiful face of an angel. His Christian conduct and his devotion to Jesus were above reproach.

But he had no military training or experience in battle. Some would doubt that he actually led the forty-thousand people under siege at Shimabara. They suspect that a council of five or six ex-samurai actually directed military operations while according respectful lip service to this "boy of divine power." This would be difficult to prove one way or the other because so many records were lost when the besieged castle was destroyed. Nevertheless, the Christian revolutionaries accepted en masse the angelic Shiro as their savior and leader.

The revolt spread. Heeding Shiro's call to arms, the Christians sped to Shimabara Castle, abandoning their villages. Those peasants not sufficiently fleet of foot were incinerated in their own homes.

Hara Castle ruins, where 37,000 Japanese men, women, and children died in defense of their faith. *Courtesy of Minami Arima-machi City Office, Education Committee*

The shogunal forces were under the command of General Itakura, who introduced a new level of savagery into the conflict. When he captured rebel children, he had them burned to death at the stake, which only served to further inflame the hostility of the adult rebels.

In the initial stages, even though they bore only spears and scythes, Shiro Amakusa's troops won battle after battle. With each successive defeat of the hated forces of the Edo dynast, the rebels captured plentiful stands of matchlocks, and these firearms brought them even more victories.

One explanation for these early triumphs was the great distance between Shimabara in Kyushu and the Shogun's capital in Edo. Sixteen days was the standard travel time. News of the *émeute* reached Edo in sixteen days, and the Shogun and his advisors took at least several more days to mull the matter over. Then their couriers—the *hikyaku*, or "flying legs"—had to make the return journey over the Tokaido to Osaka and from there by sea to Kyushu. In the meantime, there was not one *daimyo* in Kyushu who dared take military action of any sort against Shiro Amakusa and his abettors without specific orders from the Shogun in Edo.

The siege of the castle lengthened. By March the number of government soldiers had risen to over one hundred thousand, with more on their way. These soldiers surrounded the castle at a distance of four-hundred to five-hundred yards. This vast assemblage of men was divided into seven divisions, each from a fief loyal to the Shogun. (Not all were.) The fiefdoms fell to fighting among themselves while, on the castle walls, Amakusa's men cheered these internecine skirmishes.

In late March General Itakura directed that a tunnel be dug under the walls to provide an avenue of attack. This plan might have worked had not the besieged detected the sounds of excavation. Digging a hole directly down into the tunnel, the Christians began pouring feces and urine on their enemies. The approximately forty thousand souls inside the castle (the number was beginning to decrease) produced a sizable amount of human waste every day, and they were pleased to find a way to dispose of it. To say the least, this deluge inconvenienced Itakura's mole-like stalwarts.

The food supplies of the insurgents were nearly exhausted. On the 4th of April angel-faced General Shiro Amakusa led a sortie out of the castle gate and into the government camp. It was a major win for the boy general. Still, some three hundred of Amakusa's men were killed, and when their stomachs were slit open, it was learned that most of them had been living on seaweed and barley. This told General Itakura that the end was in sight. He ordered an all-out attack on the 12th of April and two days later the defenses began to crumble.

As the shogunal forces pushed into the confines of the citadel, they methodically set ablaze each structure as they came to it. In large numbers the insurrectionists were burned to death. Those Christians not inside the torched houses tried frantically to force their way into the flames to die with their comrades and families. They pushed their children ahead of them and held up the burning beams so even more could follow them. One of the daimyo dedicated to crushing the rebels wrote that he had never seen such fortitude, not even among regular samurai: "Words cannot express my admiration."

With government samurai rushing here and there, madly whacking off heads, there was no question about who had won. Sasaemon, a retainer of the Hosokawa *daimyo*, looked inside a burning hut and sighted a youth with angelic features lying wounded on the floor. The Hosokawa warrior, who knew the story of Jesus Christ, fancied that he detected a similarity between the gentle face of the injured youth and what he thought might have been the look of Jesus dying on the cross.

As the youth struggled to rise to his feet, Sasaemon cut off his head. With the head in hand, he ran out of the burning hut just as it collapsed behind him.

A harbor in the Amakusa Islands, where Christian
faith flourished in the early 1600s.

Sasaemon carried his trophy to the *kubi-jikkensho*—the place where heads were examined. Amakusa's mother (her Christian name was Martha) sat there filled with dread while being forced to look closely at all the grisly mementos. (At first, she had refused to believe that her Messiah son could be killed.) When the head taken by the Hosokawa man arrived, she looked at it, shuddered, and moaned, "Can he really have become so thin?" Shiro's head was taken to Nagasaki for public exhibition. His mother and all his family were executed.

On the instructions of the victorious *daimyo*, many heads were mounted on bamboo stakes, which had been driven into the ground of an immense field off to one side of the castle. Let that be a warning to all, the *daimyo* said, ordering that all the heads remain where they were until the ravens and seabirds had eaten their fill of the flesh on the skulls.

It must have been a grim and macabre sight, from among a historical cornucopia of such tableaux, for official sources tell us that 10,869 heads decorated the forest of bamboo stakes in that field. (This display of the heads of fallen foe was a favored activity of victorious Japanese generals. After his victory at Sekigahara on October 21, 1600, Shogun-to-be Ieyasu Tokugawa arrayed thirty-five thousand heads for display. At least that many if not more were exhibited in 1615 after the Natsu No Jin, or "Summer Campaign," in which Ieyasu defeated Hideyori at Osaka Castle and constructed the infamous "Avenue of Heads" on planks most of the way to Kyoto.)

This bloodbath wrote finish to Shiro Amakusa's rebellion and to public Christian worship in Japan. There are those who would say that violent oppression and persecution will always be vanquished in the end, but in Japan such optimism did not apply. Christianity never really recovered from its unmitigated defeat at Shimabara.

Not a sound was heard from this creed for 230 years, and even after that Christianity stagnated as a pallid, hesitant ghost of its previous self.

## References

1.   Murdoch, James. *A History of Japan*, Vol. II. London: Routledge & Kegan Paul, 1949.

2.   Morris, Ivan. *The Nobility of Failure*. Tokyo and Rutland, Vermont: Charles E. Tuttle Co., 1982.

3.   Ebisawa Arimichi. *Amakusa Shiro*. Tokyo, 1967.

4.   Pages, Leon. *Histoire de la Religion Chrétienne au Japon depuis 1598 jusqu'à 1651*. Paris, 1869–70.

5.   Boxer, C.R. *The Christian Century in Japan*. Berkeley: University of California Press, 1951.

6.   Storry, Richard. *The Way of the Samurai*. New York: Galley Press, 1978.

7.   Bunce, William K. *Religions in Japan*. Rutland, Vermont: Charles E. Tuttle Co., 1955.

## CHAPTER THIRTEEN

# Night Crawling, Eel Traps, and Retreaded Hymens

*Is it possible for there to be a connection among the above three topics? Just what is 'night-crawling' anyway? A 'hymen,' of course, is a maidenhead, but how is one of them retreaded? Well, there are logical yet strange answers to these questions.*

### KYUSHU, 1946

It was a moonless summer night in central Kyushu in the year 1946. A breeze was trifling with the surface of the shallow, clear Chikugo River.

I stood at the stern-oar of a fourteen-foot skiff, awkwardly managing to move the boat forward as needed. In the prow squatted a young man, who was following a trot-line and pulling up the attached eel traps one by one. With deft, accustomed hands he opened each trap and emptied its contents of squirming river eels into buckets in the bottom of the skiff. These he would try to sell on the morrow in the nearby town of Yoshii. His name was Kenji Tanaka and he was crippled in one leg from a war injury. Kenji was the 26-year-old son of our host, the principal of the girls' middle school, also in the town of Yoshii.

Two other eelfishing skiffs were nearby.

It was curiosity that had drawn me to this region of central Kyushu. In the course of our studies in Japanese culture and language at the University of Michigan during the just-ended war, one of our textbooks made mention in passing of the research of an American scholar by the name of John Embree, who in pre-war days had spent a season in the town of Suye-mura not far from south of where we were eel-fishing on the Chikugo River.

Scholar Embree had heard of the odd Kyushu custom of *yobai* (night-crawling) and, intrigued, had made a study of it. What he learned, and later reported in a book, captivated me. I had to go see for myself, so soon after arrival in our duty station of Fukuoka, I made arrangements to take a weekend trip to that part of Kyushu and persuaded two of my classmates, Ken Edge and Adrian (Doc) Blanchard, to keep me company. (They did not, however, see in the consuetude of *yobai* the possibilities that I discerned.)

We left our Civil Censorship Detachment unit in Fukuoka after duty hours on a Friday evening and headed south for Suye-mura. What with bomb craters and all, some of the roads were still in a state of ill-repair, so we had known we could not reach our goal that night. Accordingly, we had used an introduction from one of our fellows officers to pay a visit to Mr. Tanaka, the principal of the girls' school in Yoshii.

He was delighted to see us and have us spend the night, which was not suprising. Most Japanese were most affable to Americans in those days, especially if we came heavy-laden with C-rations and assorted potables.

For dinner that night our host regaled us with eel dishes. It was my first taste of eel, and I became instantly fond of the flesh of the slithery creatures. We had eels en brochette, barbecue-over-charcoal eels on a bed of white rice (*una-don*) and something I called, for lack of a better name, Eel Slubberdegullion. All were good, but the *una-don* was superb. Truly unforgettable.

When the dishes were cleared away from the low table in the center of the spacious *kyaku-ma* (guest room), we charged our glasses with beer in anticipation of a postprandial conversation about matters of mutual interest. I—in particular—wanted to tell Mr. Tanaka about my research project for the weekend: whether or not the custom of *yobai* (night-crawling) was alive and well in Suye-mura, a couple hours south of us.

Our host invited us most cordially to pass the remainder of the weekend in his home, but I replied, "We'd like to, Mr. Tanaka, but tomorrow morning we must press south to Suye-mura."

"Might not your business in Suye-mura be something you could just as well accomplish here in Yoshii? We are, in fact, quite a bit larger than Suye-mura, which I know well, and, if I may say so, we are far more cultured."

"We really must go on," I said to head off my comrades Ken Edge and Doc Blanchard. I could already tell that they were more interested in trying to empty the local sake vats than pursuing some nebulous pseudo-scientific endeavor to the south of us—over perilous roads, at that. Besides, Mr. Tanaka had said something about a group of female teachers from his school paying him a visit on the following afternoon. (They had heard of our arrival and wanted, I am confident, to practice their English conversation on real, living native speakers of the language.)

"A famous American scholar," I said, "discovered that the rural folk around Suye-mura practice something called *yobai*. We want to confirm that—and see how it works. Are you familiar with *yobai*?"

"Oh yes, some of the people here in Yoshii have been known to wrap towels around their faces and go night-crawling, too, but I must admit that it is more widely practiced in Suye-mura." The slight, aesthetically pleasing-looking school principal seemed disappointed that he could not persuade us to investigate *yobai* in his more cultured bailiwick.

I wondered if this fine old custom was practiced in Yoshii in the same way as in Suye-mura, so Ken Edge and I alternated in relating to the principal what we had learned about *yobai* back at the University of Michigan.

The sum of our knowledge, we told Tanaka, was that in the rice-harvesting season, the rice-growers asked for the help of friends, neighbors, and relative to bring in the harvest. They offered these temporary workers food and a futon somewhere in the reed-matted rooms of the farm house.

"Sometimes," I said, "there may be as many as a dozen futon on the floor of one room with even more along the corridors of the house. This offers endless opportunities for...what shall I say? ...hanky-panky?"

"I take your meaning, young sir," said the school principal in his charmingly accented English.

"So one or another of the country swains will, in the dark, crawl around among the futon until he finds his sweet patootie of the evening and attempts to snuggle in between the futon with her."

"If she rejects his overtures," said the quiet, stolid Doc Blanchard, taking up the story, "it will mean a serious loss of face to him, so to protect his reputation, he has the foresight to wrap a towel around his head and face."

"That way," Ken Edge broke in, " the woman can always say she did not know who she kicked out of her futon."

"Of course she *did* know who he was," I continued. "It was all just an elaborate fabrication. When the rejector and the rejected meet in the rice paddies the next day, both can pretend ignorance." I paused. "Is that the way it is done here in Yoshii as well?"

"Just about the same—with a few minor variations," Tanaka replied. "Sometimes a predetermination is made about the color of the towel to avoid mistaken identity. The traffic in crawlers can be heavy some nights, especially when there's a full moon."

Blanchard, Edge, and I entered into a debate about whether to remain in Yoshii and learn what we could about the local version of *yobai* or press on to Suye-mura on the morrow. In the midst of our wrangling, young Kenji Tanaka rose to his feet and announced, "I've got to run my eel trot-lines. Would anyone care to come along?"

It seemed to be the least we could do in partial repayment for the hospitality of the Tanaka household, and this is how I came to be standing at the stern-oar of an unsteady skiff in the middle of the shallow, swift Chikugo River.

Just as Kenji was emptying the fifth eel trap in a convenient bucket, the boat carrying Doc Blanchard and Mr. Tanaka collided with ours from the rear. Both overturned, and we all found ourselves waist-deep in the fast-flowing Chikugo. Desperately Kenji Tanaka tried to retrieve the eel buckets before all the slippery creatures made good their escape back into the river. In this, he was only partially successful, and many of the eels swam off in this direction or that; in fact, one found the bottom of my right trouser leg and decided it looked like a handy place in which to seek refuge.

As soon as he started up my leg, past my knee, and on toward my lower region, I struck out for the shore of the river about 20 yards distant.

Observing my progress cleaving through the water, Ken Edge later insisted that I try out for the next Olympic swimming team. He compared my alacrity in the water with that of the far-famed Johnny Weissmuller of the 'Tarzan' movies.

On the shore, I danced out of my trousers, flung the intrusive eel back into the Chikugo, and retreated into the Tanaka home to change into a dry *yukata* (summer robe).

The Chikugo River in Kyushu.

I was still in a state when the others returned from the eel expeditions. My erstwhile comrades were laughing gaily and making ribald remarks about being sodomized by an eel and losing one's chastity along the upper reaches of the Chikugo River.

When we had re-assembled around the low dining table and Mr. Tanaka's wife and daughters had carried in trays of more beer and sake, the school principal filled each of our glasses in turn, then said, "You American gentlemen may jest about such matters, but there truly have been cases of hymens ruptured by eels driven mad in their desperation to find an escape route."

"Get out of here," said Edge in English.

Looking startled, Tanaka started to get on his feet—until I laid a restraining hand on his arm.

"You've got to be kidding," said Blanchard.

"Not in the least, Lieutenant. In fact, one of my students who lives quite near us was deflowered one night while swimming in the nude along this very stretch of river." Tanaka shook his head sorrowfully. "The girl's loss nearly drove her father—he is the local surgeon—to distraction."

"We learned in school that the Japanese don't make a big deal about an intact maidenhead," observed Edge.

"Sometimes we don't, but this girl wanted to attend a missionary college in Kobe, where she would have been subjected to a tactile examination to determine the status of her virginity before matriculation."

"Wow," said Blanchard.

"That's right," said the principal. "Her hopes for a fine academic career would have been dashed."

"So what happened?" I wanted to know.

Tanaka-san shook his head as if to break free of his memories. "That was two years ago, and Kimiko—that's her name—is doing well in the girls' school in Kobe."

"There was no—ah, tactile examination?" I asked.

"She passed," he said with a smile, "with flying colors."

Puzzlement was written clear on our faces.

"After about a year of experimentation," Tanaka explained, "her father developed a surgical technique whereby he was able to implant a *jinko shojo-maku*—a man-made maidenhead."

"Kinda like getting a tire retreaded, eh?" said Edge.

Now it was Tanaka's turn to look puzzled.

"It's nothing, *sensei*," I said. "Pay him no mind."

"The doctor tightened the body tissues and sewed them back into their earlier position. The stiches were removed in about two weeks. By now her father has done the operation many times."

"Every time on his daughter?" asked Blanchard innocently.

"You're funny, Lieutenant," said the principal. "No, all the subsequent procedures were done on other local lasses."

"All violated by eels?" persisted Blanchard.

"No, of course not," said Tanaka testily. "I fear our lusty young men were to blame."

We left Yoshii the following afternoon without going to Suye-mura. My companions had apparently lost whatever interest they might have had in night-crawling and talked of little but restored maidenheads, or hymen retreads.

"Do you reckon we could get a patent on the technique?" asked Edge enthusiastically.

"Or at least open the first clinic in southern California to offer this kind of surgery," said Blanchard.

I left them to chatter on, but I was not to be derailed so readily. I wanted to see the habitude of night-crawling in its full glory, in its native climate, at its point of genesis. If that meant later pushing on to Suye-mura alone, so be it.

I knew I would make the trip someday—and I did.

### References

1. Embree, J.F. *A Japanese Village: Suye-mura*. London: Kegan-Paul. 1936

2.   Sex and Humanism: *Tokyo Doctor Wins Gratitude of Dolls through Operations.* Tokyo: *Shipping and Trade News*: May 13, 1963.

3.   In my files I also find an undated, unsourced clipping (it looks like *Time* or *Newsweek* type) with the heading "Artificial Virgins." It tells of a Japanese gynecologist, Dr. Kohei Matsukubo, turned plastic surgeon, who developed the *jinko shojo* operation in order to create artificial hymens—from prospective brides—or anyone feeling the need for such renewed roadblocks. The doctor explained it was done through the use of plastic or by tightening the body tissues. The article goes on to say that the surgery costs about $60 (whatever date this was) and takes only 20 minutes. The patients can go home when the local anesthetic wears off.

Dr. Matsukubo recently hosted a party to celebrate his 10,000th *jinko shojo* operation. He explained that he had dedicated himself to this mission of compassion for female suffering. He is quoted as saying, "Life is not fair to women."

But it would seem that neither Dr. Matsukubo nor the surgeon I had heard of in Kyushu had the honor of being the first to use the hymen retreading procedure. (See next reference.)

4.   Simons, G. L. *Simons' Book of World Sexual Records.* New York: Pyramid Books; 1974.
The following is paraphrased from p. 177—In the 1800's young English gallants vied with each other to deflower virgins to such an extent that a shortage developed. The answer was the "manufacture of apparently unpenetrated maidens." In extreme cases, some young girls had their maidenheads restored repeatedly, after each act of coitus with a new client. Disreputable surgeons appeared on the scene who made a specialty of what was then termed "revirginizing." Some girls were said to have been subjected to this retreading as often as 500 times.

## CHAPTER FOURTEEN

# Gun Control, Japanese Style

*The Japanese took to firearms with the fervor of a passionate lover. But after a while strangely they gave them up—and not for the reasons we of today might expect.*

## 1543–1637

In 1543 a Chinese vessel of unknown name sailed into the harbor of Tanegashima, an island forty-five nautical miles southeast of Kagoshima.

Aboard her were three Portuguese wanderers, who thereby became the first Europeans known to have landed on the shores of Japan. Two of them carried firearms—harquebuses (a heavy kind of matchlock)—and once on land they sought to replenish the ship's larder.

With a single shot one of the pair brought down a duck—an event of no particular consequence except to the duck. But the feudal master of the island, the bellicose Lord Tokitaka, chanced to witness the firing of the harquebus and the death of the fowl. Instantly, he set his heart on possessing the magical instrument that spat fire and dealt death from a distance.

Lord Tokitaka offered one thousand-taels of gold for each of the two harquebuses he had seen. His offer was accepted and for many years thereafter the name of the island—Tanegashima (Seed Island)—became synonymous with "firearm."

To pay one thousand-taels of gold for the weapon would be akin to buying a Winchester 73 rifle for $14,000 back in the 1870s—or an incalculable sum today. So eager was Tokitaka to arm his samurai with these harquebuses that he postponed his dinner that evening (although he was a renowned trencherman) and called to his feet Kimbei Yatsuita, his chief swordsmith.

When Yatsuita was kneeling before him, the Lord ordered him to forget about swords for the time being and bend all his energies to making replicas of these just-acquired fire-spitting, ear-deafening, heaven-sent instruments of war and slaughter.

Swordsmith Yatsuita set out to do as he was told, but no matter how hard and long he tried, he could not successfully replicate the spring mechanism in the weapon's breech.

Several months later, in despair, Yatsuita was seriously considering sticking one of his own swords into his abdomen to apologize to his lord and master when a Portuguese ship hove to in the stream off out-of-the-way Tanegashima. The ship carried an armorer and Yatsuita wondered if the weapons artisan might rescue him from his predicament.

The question having been asked, the armorer followed the swordsmith to his forge and examined Yatsuita's thus-far imperfect handiwork. He quickly saw what was being done wrong, but he did not want to say anything to the Tanegashima sword maker until he had discussed the matter with the captain of his ship, one Mendez Pinto.

Captain Pinto discerned an advantage to be gained for himself, so at his order the armorer showed the swordsmith the error of his ways. In return, the captain—not the armorer—received Yatsuita's seventeen-year-old daughter in recompense.

The girl was said to be lovely, but who knows how she looked at this remove in time? What is known is that she sailed off with Mendez Pinto to Portugal or parts thereabouts and never returned to her home on Tanegashima.

The residents considered her "voluntary" union with the hairy barbarian from Portugal and her departure for far-off heathen parts as a sacrifice of the highest order, although for all they knew she may have found a blissful existence awaiting her on the Iberian peninsula. They erected a commemorative statue of her on the island, which stands today.

Meanwhile, back at the forge, her father Kimpei Yatsuita, bending over his anvil and fire long hours every day, succeeding in manufacturing ten perfectly functioning harquebuses in his first year of endeavor.

The Japanese now began the race to arm themselves with something other than swords. Only six years after the importation of the first firearm, Lord Nobunaga Oda had placed an order for five hundred of them.

The alacrity with which Japan was able to manufacture superior shooting irons was partially attributable to the fact that the country was then by no means a backward nation, technologically. Japan's steel and copper were as good as, or better than, any being produced in Europe. And the copper was cheaper, so much so that in the seventeenth century Japanese copper was being exported to many countries. In iron and steel Japan could undersell England, the world's leader until that time.

And for two hundred years Japan had been the world's leading exporter of arms such as swords, halberds, and suits of armor. In 1483 alone, Japan had shipped 66,000 swords to China.

One factor contributing to the massive sales of swords was that these Japanese blades were far sharper than any others. Swordsmiths made them the way pastry cooks prepare dough for Danish pastry by folding the dough over and over again. Except the Japanese swordsmiths folded and hammered the metal so often one blade might have as many as 4,000,000 (yes, four *million*) layers.

In one demonstration witnessed by a Westerner, a sword made by the famous fifteenth-century smith Kanemoto II cut completely through a European blade, then sliced halfway through the barrel of a machine-gun with no damage to the Japanese sword.

Feudal swordsmiths would sometimes test their handiwork by slashing at a branch of a cherry tree, one of the hardest of woods. On the tang they often engraved the results: "This blade cut entirely through a six-inch cherry tree branch on such and such a date."

Occasionally, the smith arranged to have several condemned criminals kneel on a bench with their arms tied behind their heads. The swordsmith (or executioner) would take his stance and make a sidewise swipe at the criminals, waist-high. Again the results would be engraved on the tang of the sword: "On such and such a date this blade cut through the torsos of two-and-half evil-doers."

Not only did Japanese guns match those of Europe in quality, the Japanese devised certain improvements. They enlarged the caliber to enhance effectiveness. They invented a device that enabled the matchlock to be fired in heavy rainfall—a fatal defect of those weapons. They refined the erstwhile Portuguese firing mechanism by introducing an adjustable trigger-pull and a helical main spring. They made waterproof containers of lacquer for transporting the weapon and its powder. They developed a serial volley technique that kept more bullets flying more often.

ONLY THIRTY-TWO YEARS after the first firearms came ashore at Tanegashima, a decisive battle took place between the armies of Lord Oda and Lord Takeda at a place called Nagashino. The year was 1575.

Oda had brought thirty-eight thousand men with him to the tussle. Ten thousand carried matchlocks. Oda selected his best marksmen and arranged them in three ranks of one thousand each. After the first rank fired, they stepped back and the second rank took their place, then so on the third rank. The maneuver was analogous to the feared British square. It was very effective indeed.

Lord Takeda's hard-charging, sword-swinging samurai were cut down in the thousands by the alternating riflemen. After the Battle of Nagashino, the motivation to re-arm with guns grew by leaps and bounds. By late in the sixteenth century, firearms were probably more common in Japan than in any other country.

The art of gunsmithing reached the stage where some of the weapons had been used for several generations in the sixteenth and seventeenth centuries, then stored in godowns of the government. When Japan reverted to the use of guns late in the nineteenth century, these antiques were dusted off and converted to percussion weapons. They still functioned admirably.

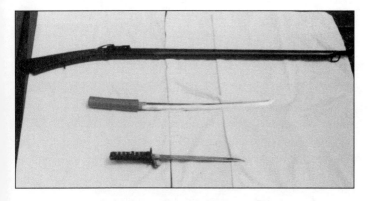

Tanegashima harquebus and heirloom swords.

And in 1904, amazingly, when the Empire went to war with Russia, thousands of these hoary firearms were converted for a second time to bolt-action rifles. Again they functioned very well, even using the more powerful gunpowder of the twentieth century.

The first heyday of the gun in Japan lasted from their introduction in 1543 until 1637 at the Shimabara Rebellion, when those weapons were used for the last time on a major scale. Even before that, in 1607, the Tokugawa Shogun ordered all gunsmiths except those in the city of Sakai (where they were too numerous and strong to attempt to control) to come together in the town of Nagahama and set up their forges. He further directed that they apply for government licenses for any firearm they proposed to manufacture.

Thereafter, the annual production had its ups and downs, from a few hundred to a mystifying 2,500 in the 1660s. But even 2,500 firearms a year is not such a huge number when one considers that the warrior class in Japan at the time of the beginning of the Tokugawa Shogunate

(1603) numbered at least two million. (In England, at the time, the comparable figure was thirty thousand.)

The Shogun's administration in Edo ordered no more guns from its gunsmiths after 1668, and by 1725 even research and development had stopped completely. In Japan, the age of the gun had faded into history, at least until the arrival of the American "black ships" in 1853.

Paramount among the reasons for Japan giving up guns was opposition from the samurai class. In battle a peasant (*heimin*) with a matchlock was equal or superior to a samurai with a sword, and to those elite warriors, this was an intolerable thought. They could not abide it.

A second reason was that the sword was regarded as the "soul of the samurai" and carried a symbolic value the firearm did not have. A third was that firearms were part and parcel of Western culture, toward which the Japanese were beginning to feel antagonistic.

Japanese battleship (Yamato) being fitted out at Kure in September 1941.
*Courtesy of Mr. S. Fukui, U.S. Naval Historical Center*

A fourth reason: the Japanese did not see themselves as engaged in a race for superior arms with potential external enemies. Japan was an isolated chain of islands that was intrinsically difficult to invade. As tough, courageous fighters, the Japanese believed they could defend their homeland adequately with conventional weapons: swords and spears.

While Commodore Perry was at anchor off Uraga, Japan, in 1853, he surveyed the antique cannon guarding Edo (Tokyo) Bay and officiously advised the Shogunal administrators that if they wanted to prevent other foreign warships (meaning those of Russia, France, and Great Britain) from forcing their way up the bay almost to the heart of Edo, they would need to forge or buy bigger and better coastal defense guns.

The Japanese decided to follow Perry's advice, and the race to arm themselves began all over again.

In 1877, the Satsuma Rebellion led by Field Marshal Takamori Saigo proved to be the last gasp of the sword. The Shogun had been dethroned and the Emperor Meiji ruled. The Meiji government opted to lessen the risk of future insurrections by making it illegal for samurai to carry swords (or to wear topknots). Enraged, droves of those swashbuckling gamecocks flocked to Saigo's banner and marched north from Satsuma (Kagoshima).

It was an unequal struggle: Saigo's swordsmen against the government's peasants carrying firearms. The denouement came when Saigo and his closest adherents resignedly committed *seppuku* on Mount Shiroyama, overlooking the city of Kagoshima.

By the Russo-Japanese War (1904–05), Japan had gained parity in firearms with the Western nations. Only thirty-six years later, in 1941, she finished fitting out the world's mightiest battleship, the *Yamato*, with its 18.1-inch guns, the heaviest ever made for warships.

### References

1.    Yumoto, John M. *The Samurai Sword*. Rutland, Vt. : Charles E. Tuttle, 1958.

2.    Inami, Hakusui. *The Japanese Sword*. Tokyo: Hakusui Sword Research Society, 1948.

3.  Perrin, Noel. *Giving Up the Gun*. Boston: David R. Godine, 1979.

4.  Ogasawara, Nobuo. *Japanese Swords*. Osaka: Hoikusha, 1970.

5.  Tsunoda, Ryusaku. *Sources of Japanese Tradition*. New York: Columbia University Press, 1958.

6.  Sansom, George B. *The Western World and Japan*. New York: Alfred A. Knopf, 1950.

7.  Draeger, Donn, and Robert W.S. Smith. *Asian Fighting Arts*. New York: Berkeley, 1974.

8.  Cooper, Michael, editor. *The Southern Barbarians*. Tokyo: Kodansha, 1971.

9.  Benedict, Ruth. *The Chrysanthemum and the Sword*. Boston: Houghton Mifflin, 1946.

10. Brinkley, Frank. *A History of the Japanese People*. New York: Encyclopedia Britannica, 1915.

## CHAPTER FIFTEEN

# Alexander Romanov: Grand Duke or Great Comedian?

*Two adventures—one humorous, the other nearly fatal— befell members of the Russian Czar's family in Japan. Both have been largely forgotten, except by a few historians.*

### TOKYO 1886

The ultra-conservative Imperial Court of Japan breaks into wild peals of laughter while listening to the speech of a stellar member of the Russian Czar's family. This seems an unlikely scenario, but here is confirmation recorded by Grand Duke Alexander in his own words:

> *Came the night of the state banquet. Placed on the right of the Empress, I gathered my courage, smiled pleasantly and addressed her in Japanese. For a second she looked astonished. I repeated my remark. She grinned. This initial success prompted me to tell her of my admiration for the progress made by Japan. It required some maneuvering on my part, and I tried to recall all the expressions used in identical cases by my Inasa friends. A strange sound came out of the Empress's throat. She stopped eating and bit her lip. Then her shoulders shook. She began to laugh hysterically. The Japanese prince seated on her left, who was lis-*

*tening to our conversation, dropped his head. Large tears*
*were streaming down his cheeks. Next moment the entire*
*table shrieked and guffawed.*

In 1886, the Grand Duke Alexander of Russia, trim and aristocratic in
his uniform, was only twenty-two but already doing his duty to God
and country by serving as a junior officer aboard a Russian warship in
Far East waters. Until 1898, Nagasaki—on Kyushu in southern Japan—
would be the winter rendezvous of the Far Eastern Squadron of the
Russian Fleet. Here the Russian warships anchored for extended periods to purchase food, coal and other supplies and to give their crews
ample shore leave.

So ample was this shore leave that many Russian naval officers made
cozy arrangements with Japanese "wives" to stave off loneliness. Each
navy had its own way of making these arrangements. French officers
apparently relied on laundrymen as go-betweens (witness the mythical
Madame Butterfly and the factual Madame Chrysanthemum), but the
Russians swore by a woman named O-Machi, who managed a high-class
restaurant in the proximate village of Inasa, off whose shores the Russian
fleet often dropped anchor.

O-Machi was a widow who was regarded as a godmother to Russian
sailors. She spoke tolerable Russian, played Russian songs on the guitar
and piano, and served fine Russian cuisine prepared by her several
Russian chefs. All she wanted, she often explained, was to make young
Russians feel at home, and her services included introducing Japanese
girls to men sailors looking for companionship.

Once the officer had settled on his futon-mate, O-machi drew up a
"marriage contract" lasting while his man-of-war was scheduled to
remain in Far Eastern waters.

Then came the "wedding dinner"—in O-Machi's restaurant, of
course—and what magnificent feasts they were: first a mammoth stur-
geon was placed in the middle of the groaning table. Next came blue
boxes filled with Beluga caviar on large blocks of ice. Then vodka and
the borscht and the *piroshki* and the other delicacies that so delighted
the Russian palate.

After all that, the binational couple settled down to the bliss of mar-
ital existence just as other men and women have done in other lands
and at other times. The only difference was that the marriage contract
lasted only one to three years, but even that may have been longer than
most American marriages survive today.

Grand Duke Alexander chose the path most of his fellow officers
took and asked O-Machi to introduce him to a suitable "bride." She
could not afford to lose face in this most delicate matter so she brought
no fewer than sixty prospects to be inspected by this peer of the
Russian realm.

At last Alexander made his choice. History does not reveal her name
or her eventual fate. How charming it would be if Alexander had sired
a child by her and that if even today there was a strain of genuine
Romanov blood running through the tiny village of Inasa, near
Nagasaki. For Alexander's bride was a native of Inasa, where the so-
called Inasa dialect was spoken—to the incomprehension of almost
everyone else.

This was the state of affairs when Alexander's far-off cousin, the
aloof Czar, thought how perfectly splendid it would be to have Alex pay
a state visit to the Japanese emperor in Tokyo.

No problem, Alexander agreed. (Besides, who could argue with the
Czar?) But the trip to Tokyo would not take place until the following
year and meantime Alexander had some living—and learning—to do.
Every evening when not on the duty roster, the Grand Duke rowed
ashore to his little blue heaven where he studied the Japanese language,
when he could spare time from his amours. Without textbooks or access
to formal classroom study, he had to learn every Japanese word that he
eventually mastered from the lips of his light-of-love. And, of course,
every word was full flavored by the disreputable, uncouth Inasa accent.

The island of Kyushu is known for strange dialects. South of
Nagasaki, in Kagoshima, the natives would be better off—even today—
communicating with outsiders in sign language rather than in their
native patois. In fact, it is said that during the long Tokugawa Era
(1603–1867) no shogunal spies ever penetrated the seclusion of
Kagoshima (then Satsuma) because their "foreign" pronunciation of

Japanese would have given them away instantly. Besides, they could not report to Edo on what they did not understand. So it was in the Inasa district.

Upon reaching Tokyo, Grand Duke Alexander was ensconced in appropriate quarters. The chief of protocol for the Japanese Imperial Court was a German from Potsdam whose preparations had been so elaborate and painfully meticulous that poor young Alexander was bored witless before the end of the first day. He had, however, the state banquet to look forward to that evening.

ONCE THE LAUGHTER at last subsided, the Grand Duke remained puzzled by his uproarious reception. Pleased, yes, but definitely puzzled. After all, he had not intended his words to be funny.

Little by little the light of comprehension began to glimmer. Emperor Mutsuhito began the waltz of words with the obligatory, "You speak our language very well, Your Highness." A prince followed with, "How many language lessons did Your Imperial Highness take?"

With a sparkle of amusement in her eyes, the lovely young Empress came more to the point. "Who was your teacher, Grand Duke?"

For the Grand Duke had spoken to the Empress and the other auto-cratic personages at the formal banquet in pure Inasa dialect—the only Japanese he knew. (Such *lèse-majesté* by a Japanese commoner would have merited draconian punishment.) To appreciate the full fla-vor of what Alexander described as the "gayest banquet in the history of the (Japanese) empire," imagine the formal banquet room in Buckingham Palace in London. The English queen has just directed that her guest's, the American president's, champagne glass be changed. The president declines with the words, "I ain't no 'and fer them fancy drinks, Liz, me gel, but a tot uv gin wud go down lawk cream, it wud."

The Grand Duke was not directly involved in the Russo-Japanese war eighteen years later, but in World War I he was named comman-der-in-chief of the Imperial Russian Air Force.

## OTSU 1891

Scarcely four years after the hilarious banquet, Alexander was followed to Japan by an even more exalted member of the Russian royal family, also twenty-two and the heir-apparent to the Russian throne. He was the Czarevitch who became Czar Nicholas II—executed by the Communists in July 1918 at Ekatarinberg, Russia.

The mustached Czarevitch and his party had landed in the south of Japan and progressed overland to the northeast through Kobe and Kyoto. Just beyond Kyoto, in the small town of Otsu, the Russian heir-apparent with his party and guides rode through the narrow streets in a parade of fifty rickshaws between double ranks of local policemen. The security was absolute, for the Japanese emperor had proclaimed, "I take personal responsibility for the Czarevitch's visit. His person shall be as sacred as my own. I answer for his safety with my own." Fine words.

The future Czar Nicholas II during his visit to Japan.

*Courtesy Nagasaki Prefectural Library*

As the rickshaw of the unconcerned Czarevitch rolled along between the serried ranks of Japanese gendarmes, one of them—a Sanzo Tsuda—aimed a murderous slash of his sword at the head of the Russian heir-apparent, whose hat was all that prevented the blow from being fatal.

Before Tsuda could deliver a second cut, the rickshaw coolie, with remarkable courage and coolness, flung himself on the vengeful Tsuda and dragged him to the ground. A second rickshaw coolie grabbed Tsuda's blade and dealt the still aggressively struggling off-duty police-man—for such he turned out to be— several severe lacerations.

Momentarily blinded and bleeding copiously from the cut on his head, the youthful Czarevitch was led to a nearby shop, where first-aid was administered, although he made light of his wound.

The uproar following the attack was nearly beyond belief. The entire nation came to a virtual halt: stores were shut, theaters closed, all work stopped. Over twenty thousand well-wishers visited the Kyoto hotel where the future Nicholas II was resting, following this gory disruption in his schedule.

A special train carrying cabinet ministers, ambassadors, officials of the court, famous physicians, and medical professors from the Imperial University left the capital for Kyoto. The Emperor himself departed Tokyo the following day for the injured visitor's bedside, after having issued an Imperial Rescript of apology to Russia (an almost unheard-of happening.)

The Kyoto telegraph office was unable to cope with the incoming traffic. Every newspaper headlined words of grief and indignation. Thousands upon thousands of ordinary citizens went to their shrines and temples to offer thanks for the deliverance of the Czarevitch. Incense burned; temple gongs sounded. In shame, the citizens of Otsu, where the attack took place, discussed changing the name of their town.

When leaving Japan the Czarevitch's ship rode heavy-laden with the mountains of gifts sent him by the ordinary people of Japan. A flotilla of Japanese warships escorted his vessel as far as the western exit from the Inland Sea.

A contemporary wag commented that if a Russian fleet and a Russian army had appeared on the horizon just then, the Japanese people might have laid down en masse and begged the Russians to forgive them and put them out of their misery.

How times change. Nowadays most Japanese have nothing but disdain for the Russians.

*Addendum:* The government of Russia rewarded the two quick-thinking rickshaw coolies with a decoration from the Czar, a cash gift of $2,500 and a pension of $1,000 a year for life—a princely sum in those times. Their own government in Tokyo also gave them medals and pensions.

Grand Duke Alexander, brother-in-law of Czar Nicholas II, also visited Japan. *Courtesy of Corbis-Bettmann*

### References

1.  Williams, Harold S. *Foreigners in Mikadoland*. Tokyo: Charles E. Tuttle, 1963.

2.  Alexander, Grand Duke of Russia. *Once a Grand Duke*. Garden City, New York: Garden City Publishing, 1931.

3.  Suzuki, Kenji. "Rokoku Kotaishi Sonan." In *Rekishi E No Shotai*. Tokyo: Nippon Hoso Shuppan Kyokai, 1980.

## Chapter Sixteen

# Z - Z - Z - Z

*The fate of the empire would ride on the shoulders of Operation Z, said the masters of the Imperial Japanese Navy. Yet the plan may have been compromised when Admiral Fukudome's flying boat crashed in a storm in the Philippines. If the Operation Z plan could be found and translated quickly, it might mean the difference between victory and defeat for the U.S.*

## The Philippines and Australia 1944

To avoid having to commit *harakiri*, Admiral Shigeru Fukudome told the Imperial navy board of inquiry that his briefcase containing the master plan for Operation Z burned in the wreck of his four-engine Kawanishi flying boat when it crash-landed in the sea after running out of fuel just short of Cebu in the Philippines. Also in question was the allegation that the Admiral had allowed himself to be captured by Philippine guerrillas in violation of the *Senjin-kun* (Combatants' Code).

Perhaps in consideration of the dire shortage of high-ranking naval officers, the board of inquiry voted three to two not to press charges against the admiral (or his companion Commander Yamamoto). The board did, however, invite the pair to spend the night in a room in the Navy Ministry "without the presence of a guard." This invitation was tantamount to a strong suggestion that Fukudome and Yamamoto cut open their bellies in expiation. Neither of the navy officers availed themselves of this gracious opportunity.

Far from being reduced to ashes in the flaming wreck of the flying boat, the plan—water-stained and with a 'Z' printed prominently on its red cover—had been delivered by guerrilla courier, submarine, and aircraft to Douglas MacArthur's headquarters in Australia. An all-out effort was made in Australia by the best American translators in the Pacific Theater to render the plan into English and urgently disseminate its contents to a strictly limited number of American generals and admirals.

Like the decoding by American navy linguists of Japanese wireless messages that enabled us to win the sea battle at Midway (June 1942), the capture and speedy translation of Plan Z was one of the two most important intelligence coups of the war in the Pacific. To understand the strange sequence of events, let's begin with the name of the plan itself: Z (called "zed" in the British Commonwealth and "*zetto*" in Japan).

When Admiral Heihachiro Togo raised the Z pennant from the mast of his flagship *Mikasa* prior to Japan's awesome victory in 1905 over what had been the Russian Baltic fleet, he had compelling precedents in mind. The flag was quartered in red, blue, black, and yellow, similar to the signal raised when the Japanese attacked the Russian fleet at Port Arthur.

It also flew in memory of Lord Admiral Horatio Nelson and his epic English victory over the combined French–Spanish fleets off Cape Trafalgar on the southeast coast of Spain (in 1805). While the shipboard bands were playing "Rule Britannia" and "Britons Strike Home," Lord Nelson took one last adoring look at the portrait of his mistress Emma Hamilton hanging on the wall of his spacious, well-appointed cabin, climbed to the deck, and ordered his flag lieutenant to make to the fleet the signal engraved even now on the heart of every English schoolboy: "England expects that every man will do his duty."

(At first, Nelson had said, "England confides that every man will do his duty," but the flag lieutenant had asked Nelson to reconsider. The word "confide" was not given in the codebook and would have to be spelled out. "Expect," on the other hand, was transmittable by one symbol in code.)

To the Japanese, ardent admirers of Britannia's navy if not its Pukka Sahib imperialism, Nelson's dictum was almost as well known. Accordingly, when Admiral Togo sent his Z pennant up the *Mikasa*'s mast, he was paraphrasing for his sailors, "The fate of the empire depends on this battle. Let every man do his utmost."

In April 1941, the Japanese navy's plan to attack the U.S. Pacific Fleet at its moorings in Pearl Harbor was given the name Operation Z. Then, when Vice-Admiral Ryunosuke Kusaka's fleet approached Hawaii in early December 1941, he ordered an exact copy of the Z pennant raised over the *Mikasa* at Tsushima Strait to be flown over his own flagship, the aircraft carrier *Akagi*.

One day after the disaster at Pearl Harbor, a British fleet set sail from Singapore to intercept Japanese convoy landings on the eastern coast of Malaya. The fleet consisted of the 36,727-ton battleship *Prince of Wales*, the 33,250-ton *Repulse*, and four over-age destroyers. It was under the command of Vice-Admiral Sir Thomas Phillips, who was known as "Tom Thumb" Phillips because he had to stand on a box on the bridge of his flagship to see over the railing. Tom Thumb's fleet was called Force Z.

Unlike Japan's victories at Tsushima Strait and Pearl Harbor (and Great Britain's at Trafalgar), the sortie of Force Z up the coast of Malaya ended in unmitigated catastrophe. Both the *Prince of Wales* and the *Repulse* were sunk, although they died such "beautiful deaths" that Japanese pilots responsible for their sinkings were inspired on the following day to fly over the spot where the enemy ships had died and drop wreaths of flowers in appreciative commemoration.

Counting on the letter Z to serve as a talisman for one more magnificent triumph, Japan used the letter again to describe its Combined Fleet Secret Operations Order No. 73, dated March 8, 1944. This was Operation Z, also named the Z Plan. It set the scene for a naval battle as decisive as Tsushima Strait and Trafalgar, that was seen as Japan's final hope to win the war.

In Tokyo, the Imperial navy staff realized that the major American thrust against the Philippines would come from the east, from the Marianas. The Z Plan spelled out how the Marianas were to be defended, what strength the Japanese had on that date, and what strength they projected having available later. Foreknowledge of the details of Plan Z would put American commanders inside the minds of the enemy's top naval brass.

Yoshikazu Yamada, a member of the ATIS team who translated the Japanese Z Plan in record time, leading to one of the two major intelligence coups of the Pacific War. *Courtesy of Harry Fukuhara*

When he attacked the Marianas en route to the Philippines, Admiral Raymond Spruance would know, for instance, that the Japanese had

nine carriers with 460 aircraft aboard as well as the number and location of the enemy's land planes available to resist the onrushing
American invasion fleet.

Actually, Plan Z was the brain-child of Japanese Admiral Mineichi
Koga, who could recite its details from memory. Based at Palau in the
Carolines, Admiral Koga knew, of course, of the devastating air raids
made on the Japanese bases of Truk and Rabaul earlier that year. Not
wanting to be separated from his forces if the same destruction was
rained on Palau, he determined to moved his headquarters to Davao, on
Mindanao in the Philippines. Two Kawanishi flying boats were alerted
to accommodate him and his staff on their journey.

Koga's chief of staff was Admiral Shigeru Fukudome. The two
would ride in separate aircraft, Koga decided, giving Fukudome a copy
of the Z Plan. Flying at night, the two giant flying boats ran into a
severe storm when they were already over the waters of the
Philippines. Admiral Koga's plane was lost and never heard of again,
although rumors persisted that Koga survived, only to later commit
*harakiri.*

Chief of Staff Shigeru Fukudome's flying boat, however, ran out of
fuel and crashed into the sea as it was nearing Cebu. Fukudome, among
the survivors, swam about in the darkness for hours, the briefcase containing Plan Z clutched under one arm, until finally he was rescued by
Filipino fishermen. Fukudome had released his hold on the briefcase
just before being rescued, but an alert Filipino sighted the briefcase
sinking slowly into the depths and retrieved it.

The fishermen turned the briefcase with Plan Z over to a band of
guerrillas, one of whom had studied in Japan and knew just enough
Japanese to recognize the meaning of the Japanese characters for "Top
Secret" on the red cover.

The commanding officer of all the guerrillas in that area, an
American named James Cushing, telegraphed MacArthur's headquarters in Australia that his band had captured top secret documents and
high-ranking Japanese officers. MacArthur's staff replied that the officers and the documents should be sent to Australia with all possible

dispatch and that a submarine was being sent into Philippine waters to take them aboard.

In the meantime, the Japanese military forces stationed in Cebu had announced that entire villages of Filipinos would be massacred if Admiral Fukudome was not immediately released. James Cushing, who had very close ties to the Filipino communities, felt he had no choice so he released the captive admiral, thereby risking and receiving MacArthur's wrath. He did manage, however, to send the Z Plan by two of his runners to the submarine rendezvous.

The runners, after several narrow escapes, were able to stand in the surf and hand over the plan—one of the most important Japanese documents ever seen by Americans during the Pacific war—to American submariners who wondered why they had been told to risk their lives for this seemingly innocuous report in a language unintelligible to them.

George (Yamashiro) Sankey, also a member of the ATIS team who translated the Japanese Z Plan. *Courtesy of Mitsuko Sankey*

Back in Australia, the staff of the Allied Translator and Interpreter Section waited with growing excitement. Colonel Sidney Mashbir, the cigar-chewing, imposing commanding officer of ATIS, ordered his top five translators to be ready: Richard Bagnall, Faubion Bowers, Yoshikazu Yamada, John Anderton, and George (Yamashiro) Sankey.

Faubian Bowers (right), also a member of the ATIS team, who later became an interpreter and aide to Douglas MacArthur (center). *Courtesy of Faubian Bowers*

As soon as the water-stained, red-backed Plan Z arrived at ATIS headquarters, its immense importance was recognized at once. This was indeed the document that Admiral Shigeru Fukudome was to swear later at the board of inquiry in Tokyo was destroyed by fire in the flaming wreck of his flying boat. (Writing in his memoirs published in

1976, the admiral still clung to his version of history. Yet, a few years after the close of the Pacific War—and long before Admiral Fukudome published his memoirs, a Japanese navy staff officer, Commander Masataka Chihaya, found the original Plan Z nestled among other documents in SCAP's Historical Section in Tokyo.)

Working without rest, the ATIS translators gave top-priority attention to completing their task. One translation dispute even forced Colonel Sidney Mashbir to cable Washington to refer the disagreement to the "highest authority locatable" in the United States.

Exactly twenty copies of the complete twenty-two-page translation were mimeographed, with Mashbir turning the crank. These copies were distributed to the highest levels of American admirals and generals who were responsible for the imminent invasion of the Marianas.

The number of U.S. lives, ships, and aircraft saved by foreknowledge of Plan Z cannot be calculated, but it is safe to say the figures would be eye-opening.

### References

1. Warner, Denis, and Peggy Warner. *The Sacred Warriors*. New York: Avon Books, 1982.

2. Toland, John. *Infamy*. New York: Doubleday & Co., 1982.

3. Toland, John. *The Rising Sun*. New York: Random House, 1970.

4. Howarth, Stephen. *Morning Glory*. London: Arrow Books, 1985.

5. Howarth, David. *Trafalgar*. New York: Atheneum, 1969.

6. Fukudome Shigeru. *Forty Years of Life in the Navy*. Tokyo: Jiji Press, 1976.

## CHAPTER SEVENTEEN

# A Kitten Battles the Traffic at the Iigura-cho Intersection

*If you confront a human baby, a puppy, and a kitten with a sudden danger, the baby will scream, the puppy will grovel and whine for mercy, but the kitten will arch its back, hiss, and prepare to defend itself valiantly.*

### TOKYO 1972

On a drizzly November day in Tokyo, instead of walking to my office next to Tokyo Tower, I hailed a taxi and told him to drive to the Iigura-cho corner, then turn right and go down past the Russian Embassy toward the Tower.

I would soon experience an unusual incident that for all its seeming insignificance would nevertheless make an indelible impression on me. Perhaps more indelible than any other I saw in my twenty-five years in Japan.

Traffic was heavy that wet fall morning, but my cab driver hardly braked at all when cornering right at Iigura. I was sitting directly behind him gazing idly at the madly speeding cars while we were in the midst of our curving maneuver. Glancing at the wet pavement of the street I spotted a brindled kitten, surely less than two months in age, squatting awkwardly amidst all those vehicles whizzing by.

The tiny cat was in my field of vision for only seconds, but long enough for me to notice that the lower half of his little body had been completely crushed and immobilized. This brave kitten was supporting his upper body on his left front leg while making boxer-like jabs at the onrushing monster enemies with his right paw.

Plainly this little feline gladiator had a strategy and fully intended to defend himself to the best of his ability against the overwhelming odds.

I yelled at the driver to stop at the corner after we completed our turn. Jumping from the cab, I dashed through the traffic, holding the frenzied honking vehicles at temporary bay with a sternly raised hand. At that moment I was functioning purely on instinct. I had no idea if the cat was in any condition to be rescued. I only knew I had to reach its side and do something.

I felt no fear of the cars narrowly missing me. All I felt (that I remember now) was a deep, black anger that we all live in a world where tragedies like this could occur, and go almost unnoticed.

Before I got halfway to my goal, however, I saw I was already too late. One car, then another had run over the kitten until all that remained of its flattened body rose no more than a half-inch above the pavement. Through the shouts and horn blasts and screeching brakes, I stumbled half-blind back to my taxi and reluctantly let the driver carry me on to my publishing company office.

During the rest of the day at my desk, I accomplished far less than I should have. My mind kept wandering and sometimes a little moisture gathered in the corner of an eye. At noon I didn't go out for lunch but sat behind my desk and looked out the window at the orange girders of Tokyo Tower. About 2 P.M. I removed the "Do Not Disturb" sign from my door and tried to complete some of the more essential functions expected of me.

Late that afternoon the sun came out and about 6 P.M. I set out to walk home, as was my custom when the weather was fair. I knew I would pass the Iigura-cho intersection along the way, and steeled myself for what I might see.

But there was very little left. The rain and the hundreds—probably thousands—of cars that had sped across that tragic spot left almost nothing: a few strands of fur stuck to the pavement. A faint reddish tinge maybe the size of a baby's hand. By the following morning even those would be gone. There was nothing to be done so I walked on home.

"A cat backed into a corner becomes a tiger"—Aleksandr Lebed

*Drawing by J. R. Britt, Magnolia, Texas*

I was subdued and withdrawn all evening. My family commented on this, so finally I told them what I had seen. One of them said, "But it was only a kitten."

Ah, but what a kitten.

I tried to imagine the courage it took for that tiny creature, with its final breaths and in terrible pain, to continue fighting off the huge metal monsters that were attacking it in such numbers.

It was a death scene—and a brave spirit—I can never, oh God, forget.

# CHUKEN HACHIKO: THE FAITHFUL DOG HACHIKO

*As a postscript to the feline story here's a canine
chronicle as a counter-balance.*

## TOKYO 1925

As a culture, the Japanese are not consistently kind to animals, not
even dogs. The author has seen as much cruelty to our furry friends—
probably more—in Japan as elsewhere, although the Japanese cannot
begin to compare with certain other Asians in their fiendish, depraved
practices toward animals.

Therefore, it is all the more inspiring to tell the story of Hachiko, a
pure-bred Akita. (Hachiko would be translated as Prince Eight or perhaps Companion Eight.)

Since loyalty is prime among Japanese virtues, Hachiko is far and
away the best-known dog in Japan. His owner was a professor at the
Imperial University in Tokyo who lived in Shoto, an upscale neighborhood in Shibuya Ward. It was Hachiko's wont to accompany his
master every morning from his home to the not-distant commuting
station of Shibuya and to meet him there on his return every
evening.

But one tragic day Professor Eisaburo Ueda died while away from
home. Hachiko still went faithfully to the station, but Professor Ueda
never got off any of the electric cars. This was in May 1925.

The dog continued to make his daily pilgrimages to the station until
the professor's heirs sought to separate the large, brown dog from his
scene of bereavement by entrusting him to relatives in Asakusa, a distant section of Tokyo.

Well, the move did not deter Hachiko in the least. He still set out
every day to make his trek to far-off Shibuya Station. Out of pity for
the lonely dog, Professor Ueda's heirs found him a compassionate
domicile in Yoyogi, much closer to where Ueda had caught his electric
train in the morning.

Hachiko resumed his custom of walking to the station and waiting patiently as train after train arrived—and departed. He became known and loved by a great many among the throngs who passed through Shibuya Station daily.

Statue of the "faithful dog Hachiko" in the Shibuya district. "Ever faithful, ever waiting..." *Courtesy of Kazutsugu Araki*

In 1934, Hachiko sat and watched—perhaps bemused—as Professor Ueda's granddaughter unveiled a bronze statue of him. Engraved on the monument were the Japanese words "Chuken Hachiko"—Hachiko, The Faithful Dog. Now there would be two Hachikos waiting in front of the station: one metal, the other fur and bone.

The metal lasted longer than the fur—but not much longer. After ten years of patient waiting, Hachiko died on March 8, 1935, and his bronze statue was melted down for its metal during the Pacific War that began in 1941.

HACHIKO IS NOT the only dog, of course, who has waited years for a master who never returned. In Scotland, beginning in 1858, a Skye terrier named Greyfriars Bobby waited staunchly by his master's grave for fourteen years.

Spells of inclement weather prompted the good people of Edinburgh to build him a shelter and insure his daily bread. When Bobby died in 1872—at the master's graveside, of course—he was buried next to Jock Gray, the sheep herder who had befriended him so long ago.

And outside Fort Benton, Montana, stands a memorial to a collie that waited five and a half years at the depot for another sheep herder. No one remembered ever seeing the dog until his constant presence at the railroad station came to the local residents' attention. The dog answered to the name Shep so locals theorized the dog had belonged to one of the many men who herded sheep in that area. They believed that after the shepherd died, his body was shipped—by rail—back east and that Shep had followed the coffin to the depot, then could go on no farther.

The dog stayed in the cool shade under a loading dock in the summers and next to a coal-burning stove inside the station during the harsh Montana winters. He could hear approaching trains in the distance before humans could and was always out on the platform whenever a train puffed in. After studying all the detraining passengers, Shep would search up and down the cars as if looking for someone else.

On January 12, 1942, Shep was run over by one of the trains he had come to meet. The railroad people buried him on a bluff from where his spirit could watch all the trains come and go. They built a memorial for him, and many came to visit the grave.

But eventually the trains passing Fort Benton and the visitors to Shep's grave grew few and fewer. The monument over the faithful collie fell into disrepair.

In Italy, on December 30, 1943, one Carlo Seriani caught a bus to go to work but instead kept an appointment with death—in the form of an air raid. A white mongrel named Fido waited at the bus stop for

Seriani to return, but of course he did not. Fido went back to the bus stop every night thereafter to continue his vigil. At last, fifteen years later, schoolchildren found Fido still waiting there—in death as in life.

AFTER THE PACIFIC WAR Hachiko's bronze statue was replaced and has become Shibuya's most famous landmark. It stands right in front of the station, and many people use the statue as a place to meet. Hachiko might be pleased to know that if his dear Professor Ueda should ever be resurrected and return to Shibuya, he would find at least the image of his staunch friend still waiting for him.

Some cynics sneer that Ueda's pedigreed Akita journeyed to Shibuya station daily not to greet the professor but to receive the handouts given him by nearby shopkeepers. I prefer to believe otherwise. After all, Hachiko was fed good victuals at home so why should he make the arduous and dangerous (Shibuya streets were crowded with vehicles even then) journey just for some snacks tossed to him by shopkeepers.

Mounted version of Hachiko.
*Courtesy of Mainichi Newspaper*

How can dogs be so faithful to humans when our treatment of them is so uneven and sometimes cruel? Why has this animal always been regarded as our best friend?

Maybe he just likes us… although God only knows why.

### References

1.  "Chuken Hachiko Monogatari" (The Tale of Faithful Dog Hachiko). *Josei Jishin* (Tokyo), June 2, 1987.

2.  Wallace, Irving, et al. "Greyfriars Bobby." *Parade Magazine* (New York), November 8, 1981.

## CHAPTER EIGHTEEN

# What Food These Morsels Be

*The food editor of* House Beautiful *magazine praised the culinary art of Japan as the best of the twenty-nine countries she had surveyed. But many visitors turn away in disgust from raw fish, seaweed, baby octopus and salted trout guts. Say what you will, there is no doubt that Japanese food is different… and, well, a bit strange.*

JAPANESE FOODS developed totally apart from any influences from Western cuisine. Even when European sailing vessels called at Japanese ports with considerable frequency, they brought with them few, if any, of their native foods, considering the time the ships needed to reach the shores of Dai-Nippon.

Left to their own devices, then, it seemed the Japanese had set out to express their national originality by accustoming themselves to some of the weirdest (to Westerners) dishes imaginable. And over the centuries, becoming fonder of what was readily available in their archipelago, they became addicted to it. Among the major nations of the world it is unlikely that any other people crave their own home-grown, homemade sustenance with the relentless devotion of the people of Japan.

The reaction of many foreign visitors to Japanese victuals, however, ranges from heart-felt, shuddering revulsion to ecstatic encomiums of shrill praise. The *House Beautiful* food editor cited above was referring to the kind of Japanese food served in first-class restaurants in the larger cities, where meals can cost the diners dearly. (To take his family out for a class-A dinner could cost the average office worker a week's wages.)

Aside from the sick feeling when the bill arrives, the revulsion felt by many American visitors first coming to grips with Japanese food is caused by dishes like vinegared sparrows of Wakayama, salad made with raw cartilage of pig's ear, sweet and sour sexual organs of ox, and jellied turtle-blood saké cocktails. Or crimpled snake meat, vinegared grasshoppers of Akita, fried bee grubs, pickled cherry blossoms, and sliced ovary of pig with mushrooms. Or fried red ants dipped in chocolate, smoked frogs, cooked newt with vegetables, and oiled cockscombs (for bed-wetting children). Or salted entrails of trepang, soup with sex organs of rooster, horsetail, hard-boiled mantis and centipede, frizzled earthworm, smoked silkworm larva, braised cow's hoof, smoked millipedes, mashed sea slug, pickled octopus eyes, fish bowels, and unripe gonads of sea urchins.

These above bizarre dishes are admittedly favored mainly by those whom the Japanese themselves call *getemono-gui*: people who hanker after bizarre food. But even among the more common foods one can find items that serve nearly as well: fish-eye soup (Emperor Hirohito enjoyed this), broiled sparrows with head, raw fish artistically garnished with seaweed and bean curd, dried squid (which the Japanese chew as we would gum), pickled seaweed, baby octopus served whole, leech marinated in saké, fern fiddleheads, sweet bean jelly laced with snake blood, brandied fish heads in pipkin, sea snails, peanut butter tofu, whale steak, young grass *kinton* (mashed sweet potatoes with sweetened chestnuts), and tender green maple leaves.

Part of the difficulty in presenting such delicacies lies is in their translation. An imaginative translator working with a competent public relations expert could probably increase the degree of acceptance of Japanese food by American visitors. Because the lower-echelon Japanese who write menus in English are usually limited to straight dictionary (meaning uninspired) translations, they produce mouth-watering gems like "dried gourd shavings" and "strips of fish skin and guts prescalded in boiling water" and "hot turtle soup including little eggs from the womb."

These menu writers might borrow a page from the notebook of an American advertiser who suggested that poisonous puffer or globefish be marketed under the name "sea squab." Surely someone could find a more palatable description for the tasty vegetation of the ocean bottom than simply "seaweed."

While some visitors are nauseated and a few wax lyrical, the average foreign reaction to Japanese food is hesitation and doubt and a total lack of enthusiasm. To many, the Japanese diet is bland, low in fat and sugar, and lacking in protein. They drink their green tea without sweetening and eat their rice without sugar, butter, or milk. They prefer simple fruit or a bowl of plain rice with hot tea poured over it to a sweet dessert. Upon coming home from school in the afternoon, their children ask for a tangerine or rice-crackers or a handful of vinegared rice instead of a candy bar or a dish of ice cream or a slice of bread with jam and peanut butter.

For breakfast, the Japanese usually eat steamed white rice, seaweed, a pickled vegetable (such as radish, eggplant, turnip, cucumber, spinach, or Chinese cabbage,) and perhaps a small slice of grilled fish or fried egg. For lunch, rice again predominates: a bowl topped with curry or in a lunchbox along with a few bites of vegetables and fish tucked in one corner. For dinner, they may enjoy more variety, but rice will again prevail, together with one or two pickled or briefly cooked vegetables, seaweed, a clear soup (clear so the diner can see the artistic offerings therein, such as tiny whole shrimp floating free or vegetables cut in the shape of flowers and possibly a nugget of grilled fish).

I may be erring on the generous side, but even so, Japanese food must benefit its devotees: their incidence of coronary disease is about half of Americans, and their blood- cholesterol level averages 150 compared to 225 for Americans.

Very few Japanese get fat (with the exception of sumo wrestlers, who do so deliberately). Short and stocky, yes, but few really fat people. So few, in fact, that the fleshy ones are nearly always congratulated, regarded as persons who must be financially successful. (Or else how could they afford to eat that much and work so little?) A large stomach, for example, is called a *juyaku-bara*: the stomach of a company director.

For several of my years in Japan, I was considerably overweight, and I can tell you it was a long time before I could pretend indifference to having Japanese constantly say to me, "*Suwado-san wa jitsu ni futotte imasu, ne!*" (You certainly are fat, aren't you, Mr. Seward!) A very long time, indeed.

To continue with bizarre foods, we find ashes of burnt newt (a prized love potion), snapping turtle soup, pit viper hamburger, tempura-ed chrysanthemum leaves, abalone rectums, live tiger shrimp, and the sperm of red snapper.

Let's remember, however, that the Japanese have no monopoly on odd nutrients. The Chinese still relish monkey brains taken from a just-killed young simian. The top of the skull is sawed off and the delighted diners fall to with silver spoons while the brains are still warm and pulsating. And the Coahuiltecan Indians of the American Southwest doted on spiders, lizards, and deer dung. On feast days one of their main side-dishes was called the Second Harvest: whole seeds, grains, and similar edibles carefully picked out of dry human and animal feces.

WHY IS JAPANESE FOOD so different from any other? Besides being dominated by rice, it is a cuisine in which the appearance of the food as it is served ranks in importance with its taste and nutritive value. To some, the appearance may even be more important.

The unchanging diet of the Japanese during many centuries must have motivated them to give thought to the appearance of the food to relieve the triteness of the rice, fish, *miso* soup, and pickled vegetables. This sameness was unavoidable given the economy and the limited agricultural resources of the archipelago; the people have never been able to give much thought to what we might call a balanced diet. A Japanese ate to fill his stomach from the limited selection offered. That necessity became habit that ossified with the passing centuries.

But as economic conditions improved and the Japanese could buy other kinds of food, they were willing during the period of Westernization in the Meiji Era and also during the postwar Americanization period to experiment with Western comestibles. But by and large they found them unsatisfying, although admittedly the consumption in Japan of bread, milk, coffee, ice cream, and red meat does inch up year after year. Even in the case of rice, from which the world at large gets eighty percent of its calories, most Japanese know bread is more nourishing. While one pound of bread and one pound of cooked rice have about the same caloric content, the bread has four times more calcium, twice as much Vitamin B2, and three times more protein.

Because of the emphasis on rice and a few *okazu* (side-dishes), the Japanese have some undeniable health problems. Their stomach cancer rate is high, and all vitamins except C are thought to be from fifteen to thirty-five percent deficient, resulting in a tremendous market in Japan for supplemental vitamin pills and drinks.

Even so, the Japanese today live longest of the major races of the world, and can probably thank their diet. The Japanese preference for fish and chicken over beef and pork and for fruit and short-cooked or pickled vegetables, while ingesting fewer fats and simple carbohydrates such as sugar and refined flour, has blessed their men with an average life span of seventy-six years and their women with nearly eighty-three years.

The Japanese breakfast versus the American is a graphic example: Americans may indulge themselves with cereal covered with sugar and cream or milk, pancakes with butter or syrup, eggs fried in fat, buttered toast, bacon or ham or sausage, buttered sweet rolls, and coffee with sugar and cream, while the Japanese eat rice without butter or sugar, *miso* soup (high in protein), broiled fish, pickled vegetables, and a few paper-thin dried and toasted sheets of iodine-rich seaweed, of which the Japanese eat about fifty billion sheets yearly.

Designed to pleasure the eye and the esthetic senses, Japanese food is artistically laid out on exquisite china and chromatic lacquerware that may be polygonal, triangular, square or shaped like leaves or fans.

The whole concept of dinnerware in Japan is startlingly different from that of the West. For one thing, there is no equivalent to the single large dinner plate holding the main course and vegetables. Instead, they may have two to four smaller dishes of varying colors, designs, and shapes. The standard Western dinner plate once evoked these angry words from the poet Jugaya:

> *"The European meal*
> *where every blasted plate*
> *Is round...."*

Further, the whiteness of Western dishes and the table linen remind the Japanese of a sickroom, mortuary, or surgical amphitheater: the antiseptic appearance of the dishes, the shroud-like tablecloth, the array of knives and forks that resemble surgical instruments and the flower arrangements that look like floral offerings on the tombs of the dead.

The table-color scheme, how the dishes are arrayed, and the seasonal significance of certain foods stimulate Japanese appetites. Tiny boats, for example, are minutely fashioned from bamboo sprout hulls, their sails of paper-thin cucumber slices with toothpicks for masts. Hard-boiled eggs are tinged pink or green to blend or contrast with the colors of other foods. Bits of greenery—parsley and maidenhair—are adroitly mounted here and there with a calculating eye.

Another feature of Japanese food is the extensive use of the available materials. During the thousand years that the meat of four-legged animals was off-limits, the Japanese learned to harvest the sea of an incredible variety of fish and plants. While prime bottom land grew rice and vegetables and the fields on the lower slopes fruit and tea were harvested, the Japanese turned to their mountains to discover an extensive edible array of leaves (maple and chrysanthemum), sprouts (bamboo and ginger), roots (lotus), bulbs (as lily), fungoid growths (mushrooms), pepper tree buds, fern fronds, and so on.

Still another Japanese characteristic is the care given by farmers to raising their produce. I have seen many pear, peach and apple orchards where each fruit is painstakingly wrapped in paper to prevent blemishes and ward off insects, and slope after slope of strawberry plants covered at night and uncovered in the morning only after the sun is high enough to warm them. There are fields of watermelons with forests of stakes giving the date when each melon should be picked. After harvesting, the Japanese farmer continues to exercise the same care in packing his yield for shipment to market so as little bruising weight lies on top of each piece as possible.

Other features of the islands' cuisine include prevalent use of vegetable oils instead of animal fats in cooking, exotic soup stocks (made from dried bonito, kelp and laver), unusual dipping sauces (such as soy sauce with grated fresh ginger or soy sauce and lemon juice garnished with finely chopped scallions), the relative infrequency of ovens in homes, the rare use of canned foods (which are mainly regarded as sustenance for camping trips and sea voyages only), the brief cooking time for vegetables, and—with a few exceptions—a failure to insist that food be served hot.

Within the limits of their traditional diet, the Japanese can be very self-indulgent, as if after centuries of culinary austerity, they have told themselves, "Circumstances have forced us to subsist mostly on rice, vegetables, *miso* and occasionally fish, but to compensate for these sacrifices (which, of course, may no longer be recognized as such), we will pamper ourselves by being very critical and selective within those limits."

At a typical family meal, there is seldom any audible lamenting for a good steak in lieu of the small mackerel broiled over a gas burner, but instead a continuous round of comments about how good the rice feels to the tongue and how "our *bettarazuke*" (pickled radish) compares with Mrs. Komori's down the street.

IN MICROCOSM, the saga of beef in Japan is like the story of Japan itself since it illustrates how the Japanese can embrace one foreign philosophy, cleave to it devotedly, then cast it aside for another, all the while tailoring—and often improving—the import to fit their own preferences.

That cattle have lived in Japan for a long time is evidenced by bones found in tumulus mounds from the Jomon and Yayoi cultures and from the Kofun Period. Some of these mounds or tombs date back to thousands of years before Christ. Although it is not known exactly when the inhabitants of the archipelago began eating the flesh of these and other hoofed animals, it is certain that beef was eaten if not daily at least occasionally during the early centuries of the Christian era. Otherwise, the Emperor Temmu—influenced by the recently imported religion of Buddhism—would not have found it advisable in A.D. 675 to issue an edict forbidding his people to eat cattle, horses or monkeys. (Monkeys?)

Not until the ninth century, however, did these Imperial exhortations and precepts begin to seep down to the level of the peasants who at last turned as one to fish as a substitute for the quadrupeds.

A Japanese meal on display in a restaurant's window.

Clearly, this didn't occur overnight, but eventually, the taste for beef in Japan was replaced by revulsion even at the thought of its consumption and horror at the thought of slaughtering the faithful beasts who had shared for years the farmer's lonely toil in the fields and paddies. From this choice emerged a dictum that gained wide currency: "Never eat anything you would not kill yourself."

Admirably practical, this dictum also afforded each person some flexibility. Most would kill a fish without a thought, so fish consumption was permitted, but those same persons would not kill a cow or a horse and maybe not even a pig, so the flesh of these creatures was forbidden. The flexibility, I suppose, came in the case of fowl, for one might kill a chicken for a special dinner and not let this fowl murder diminish appetite, while the next person might cringe at the prospect, preferring to subsist on rice and pickled radish.

Then came American Commodore Matthew C. Perry, who reached the shores of Japan in 1853 and lost no time requesting the local magistrate to sell his fleet sixty head of cattle and two hundred chickens.

Puzzled, the magistrate asked, "Since it is clear you do not intend to raise cattle and chickens aboard your ships, what is it that you intend to do with them?"

"Why, we'll eat them, of course," Perry replied with fetching frankness.

Shocked and nauseated, the Japanese turned their pale faces away for a moment of inner contemplation of man's inhumanity. Then, strengthened in spirit, they lectured the Americans, pointing put that "cattle are creatures useful to man because they help farmers in their daily toil."

The Americans riposted that they could not see why cattle could not help man both in the fields *and* in the kitchens.

According to one record, the magistrate replied, "So that is how you Americans repay those who serve you: by eating them?" Then he added, "We will never cooperate with your cruel wish to kill and eat such creatures."

But God—or Buddha—is on the side of the general with the larger battalions, and the monstrous black cannon on those ominous black ships in the bay were pointed right at the magistrate's tent and samurai guards, so the sixty cattle were rounded up from some shocked farming families and sent to their doom.

If the Japanese thought this was the end of the matter, they were in grievous error, for then came U.S. Consul Townsend Harris, the "barbarian" portrayed in the motion picture *The Geisha and the Barbarian* featuring John Wayne in one of his unlikelier roles.

A somewhat fleshy man whose travels and inclinations had made him a gourmandizer, Harris tried to set a fine table. However, he quickly realized that, as he wrote in an early letter "the only animal food used by the Japanese are Fish and Poultry. There is not a Sheep or Goat in all Nippon, and the few Bullocks that are kept are used for burden or the plough and are never eaten." He then prevailed upon his hosts to provide him with substitutes, so that in another letter he was able to report, "I am now supplied with wild Boar's flesh, which animal abounds in the Hills. ...I am occasionally furnished with some delicate Venison, fine large Hares, and Golden Pheasants equal to any in the world."

During those centuries when eating the flesh of four-legged animals was criminal, some—perhaps many—Japanese circumvented the prohibition by calling venison and boar by such euphemisms as *yamakujira* (mountain whale), which must be why Townsend obtained such meats early in his stay without much hassle.

While "mountain whale" may have satisfied the American consul's protein requirements quantitatively, he still hankered after beef—and in the fullness of time, he got it.

For whatever reason, Harris did not note that eventful date in his diary, but his Japanese hosts could never forget it. Although they did not record the name or breed of the first cow to become a martyr down the "barbarian's maw," they engraved these words on a monument eventually erected there.

> THIS MONUMENT, ERECTED BY THE
> BUTCHERS OF TOKYO IN 1931, MARKS
> THE SPOT ON WHICH THE
> FIRST COW IN JAPAN WAS
> SLAUGHTERED FOR HUMAN CONSUMPTION
> (EATEN BY HARRIS AND HEUSKEN)

Heusken was a Dutchman who served as the U.S. consul's interpreter, since his native tongue was much better known in Japan than English in those times.

The wedge was in the door.

This Rubicon behind them, the Japanese watched Harris smack his lips and began to wonder if the meat of their beloved cattle could be as good as he made it seem.

Which Japanese took the first audacious bite is not known, but he must have had as much courage as that other man back in history's dawn who ate the first oyster—or the first egg. In any case, the good news spread. Many Japanese—believing in the saying *doku wo kuwaba sara made* (as well hanged for a sheep as a lamb)—plunged ahead with both consumption and preparation of beef. By the middle years of the next decade, the 1860s, butcher shops could be found up and down the Tokaido, the Eastern Sea Road. These beefmongers sold their wares mostly to the hard-working porters or bearers who carried palanquins up and down the three-hundred-mile highway between the Shogun's seat of government in Edo and the Imperial capital of Kyoto.

Other ports beside Shimoda were being opened to foreigners, who within five months of their arrival in Kobe, for instance, were able to purchase ample beef in local stores. The butchers, most of whom were foreigners with Japanese apprentices, advertised frequently in the embryonic English press, as, for example, in the 23 April 1868 edition of *The Hyogo News*: "Prime ox beef, vegetables and Fresh provisions at the lowest rates."

In the following month, the editor of the same journal editorialized that a "Cattle Yard" should be built to solve the problem of the "cattle tied up in our principal thoroughfares, making both day and night hideous with their bellowings, to say nothing of the filth they leave behind them."

In 1872, the young Emperor Meiji stated that he "considered the taboo against meat to be an unreasonable tradition." He went on to point out that while there might still be those who considered beef-eating to be flighty and even sacrilegious, he felt that this kind of thinking delayed the progress of civilization.

The Meiji Emperor's writ worked much faster than the Emperor Temmu's, and in short order, his imperial judgment was translated by the man on the streets to mean, "He who does *not* eat beef is uncivilized."

How the wheel had turned! In 1853 the Americans were barbarians for eating beef; twenty years later, those Japanese who did not consume beef were the barbaric ones.

First, the trickle had become a stream; now the stream was becoming a comparative torrent. Although some Japanese still held out against eating cows, many others, regarding beef eating as a sure sign of advanced cultural attainments, strove zealously to demonstrate their sophistication.

About this time or not long thereafter, the Japanese decided that if the Western custom of eating cows was a good one worthy of emulation, then it must follow that foreign cows were superior to those that had been pulling plows through paddy mud all these years in Japan. Japanese bovine stock would have to be improved by foreign bulls. Nothing else would do.

Reminiscent of the influx of the lusty GIs into Japan right after the Pacific war, foreign bulls flooded into the islands during the last several decades of the nineteenth century, broadcasting their semen far and wide.

Chewing their cuds, the native female bovines accepted these bullish attentions with equanimity. The Shorthorn, Devon, and Simmenthal (from Switzerland) bulls dominated the imports, siring some curious crossbreeds with the help of the black native cows as well as the brown or mottled ones who traced their roots to Korea and southeast Asia.

In 1900, however, the government decided that this blind adoration of foreign cattle was excessive and had to be curbed, because deformities were appearing from the so uncontrolled bovine intermarriages. Order came quickly from chaos and cattle breeding fell under the influence of sane guidelines. A number of native breeds evolved—the Omi,

Kobe, Matsuzaka, Nambu, Echigo, Kaijima, inter alia—but the Tamba-Tajima reigns supreme today.

These cattle are raised in the hilly pastures of Tamba-Tajima, which is in the north of Hyogo Prefecture, and fattened at nearby granaries in the suburbs of Kobe. They now comprise about eighty percent of all Japanese cattle. Probably the world's best, the red meat of the Tamba cow, marbled with creamy fat, is marvelously tender and flavorful. Many world-class food authorities have pronounced it so.

How did the Japanese in only a hundred years or so transform themselves from a race that found the mere thought of swallowing a bite of dead cow meat singularly repellent into a nation that has developed the production and preparation of beef to possibly the highest level ever achieved?

The underlying principle motivating and directing Japanese efforts and success has been that beef eating, brought to them by a materialistically richer culture and sanctioned by their revered Emperor Meiji, was something more than just another way to fill one's stomach. Indeed, because of the circumstances of its introduction, it was so extraordinary that the cattle deserved to be raised with painstaking care and the beef consumed when one was financially qualified for this exotic luxury, with due respect. Without question, quality would supersede quantity.

Even if there had been space in Japan for America's wide-open ranges and great trail herds pressing toward railheads and markets over dusty trails, that scene would not have suited the Japanese conception. Instead, their cattle would be raised in twos and threes and fours by farmer folk who could give each head the attention it deserved. Beef production in Japan would be a cottage industry, not a vast operation.

Nowadays Japan has three main centers of beef production: Matsuzaka, Omi, and the area near Kobe—although, of course, cattle are raised everywhere in the islands. The practice in each area varies somewhat, but generally two-year-old calves are bought in other prefectures and shipped to one of the three main centers where they are fed on farms for two years to give their flesh the right muscle tone.

At the age of four, the beeves retire and enter a six-month fattening period.

Even before that, the attention they receive attests to the regard in which they and their flesh are held. In many instances, they are sheltered in sheds built onto the farmhouses. In hot weather electric fans keep them cool. On cold winter nights they may be covered with padded quilts—quilts maybe even taken from the beds of shivering daughters. They are fed rice, rice bran, beans, roughage, bean cake, hay, barley and fermented fodder. If their appetites decline, they are given beer and distillery lees. They are massaged for fifteen minutes or so three times every day after being sprayed by 100-proof *shochu* (low-class distilled spirits) to even out lumpiness and introduce the marbling effect—called *shimofuri* (fallen frost) in Japanese—into their flesh. If the fat becomes excessive, they may be put on a diet of white rice.

Considering the uneven past, you have to wonder what the future holds for beef-eaters in Japan. In the U.S., where 100,000 head of cattle are slaughtered every day, the consumption of their flesh has fallen off twenty percent in recent years, due to rising costs and the public's desire to reduce saturated fat in their diets.

In Japan the number of cattle has been decreasing as consumption out-paces the replacement of stock. Already the government has concluded that Japan would be better off economically to import all its beef while using land previously given over to pasture or grain cultivation.

Political considerations make this difficult, because the former outcasts, the pariahs of Japan—those called the *shin-heimin*, or New Citizens—are largely involved in slaughtering cattle, tanning hides, manufacturing leather shoes, and so on. They have so much political clout these days that districts in which they are numerous are said to have far superior classroom facilities compared to ordinary Japanese. While these New Citizens aren't exactly in the habit of spilling into the streets and manning the barricades, they do resort to some rather extreme measures to bring pressure on their political representatives. They have a fearsome if small lobby and fight nail and fang to prevent foreign beef importation on a large scale.

I have seen beef on sale in Japan for as much as $50 a pound. If beef stocks continue to diminish against a background of moderate inflation and the New Citizens continue to foil attempts to import beef in significant quantities, the only way prices can go is up—until the day when the Japanese draw the line and begin to reflect longingly on those halcyon days before the advent of the barbarian beef-eaters.

No one seriously expects the Japanese to abandon within the next one or two decades a taste and an art so assiduously obtained, but beyond that the future could even hold a reversion to those times people ate anything they could not bring themselves to slaughter personally.

The Japanese derive almost half their total protein intake from fish. Americans eat only about twelve pounds of fish a year. With Japanese fishing boats ranging farther and farther to find adequate catches, and with growing restrictions on taking certain species, costs are rising and the less privileged can't eat fish as often as their tastes might dictate.

Raw fish (*sashimi*) has doubtless done more than any other single food to turn foreigners against Japanese cuisine. Our first consul in Japan, Townsend Harris, noted in his diary with alarm, "Among the refreshments offered me were *living* fish," and his attitude has been handed down unchanged to succeeding generations of American visitors, most whose minds are simply closed on the subject. They will not even taste *sashimi*. They are positive they could not possibly like it. That untold millions of fellow humans do like or even love raw fish does not matter to them: a closed mind is a closed mind.

Nor do they consider that Americans eat more raw shellfish in the form of oysters than the Japanese do. Or that the Germans and the Dutch relish raw tuna as well as raw beef. Or that the Italians and the Greeks salivate over raw octopus and squid. Moreover, the Japanese do not eat just any fish raw. Only selected parts of certain prime ocean (not river or lake) fish are taken into the stomach uncooked. Even then the fish must be extremely fresh and dipped in soy sauce mixed usually with horseradish. In this condition *sashimi* doesn't have what foreigners describe with so much disdain as a "fishy" smell or taste.

*Fugu* is variously translated as blowfish, globefish, puffer fish, balloon fish, and moon fish. It is a tiny creature that inflates itself into a balloon-like shape when caught. Eaten both raw and cooked, it has a delicate, elusive flavor, often leaving the lips numb, much as after eating an unripe persimmon.

*Fugu* ovaries and liver contain a deadly, hard-to-isolate poison called tetrodotoxin that kills two hundred Japanese in an average year. (In 1947, the peak postwar year, the number of deaths reached 470.) Skilled chefs, who must be specially licensed, cut out the poisonous parts under running water, so *fugu* eaten in reputable restaurants is almost (an uneasy word) always safe; most deaths occur in fishermen's families who prepare their own *fugu*.

The *sashimi* of one valued species, the tiger *fugu*, costs five dollars an ounce. *Fugu* testis mixed with hot saké is drunk by eager seekers after lost virility.

IN PLACE OF a sweet dessert, most Japanese prefer what they call *sappari shita mono*: something plain and light, a dish neither cloying nor heavy. *Ochazuke* fills this need. In its simplest form, it is hot tea poured over a bowl of rice, sometimes thatched with finely crumbled seaweed and one or two bites of pickled vegetable, but it can be much more elaborate. One restaurant in Tokyo, the Hyohantei, offers fifty varieties of *ochazuke* but in all of them the essential ingredients, tea and rice, remain the same. The variety depends on what kind of chopped or ground food is used with or in place of the seaweed. Where an American would order ham and eggs after a late-hours party, a Japanese would choose *ochazuke*.

MORE THAN 700 varieties of rice are cultivated in the world, of which the Japanese raise 44, although they vastly prefer one: *mochi-gome* (a glutinous, short-grain version). They raise 4,220 pounds of rice per acre of paddy land, the world's highest rate of production. But where it takes only 60 man-hours to grow and harvest one acre of rice in the highl mechanized San Joaquin Valley of California, it takes the Japanese nearly 700. Each American eats seven pounds of rice a year, compared to 184 for Japanese.

Rice is the national delicacy of Japan, one of whose names (*Mizuho-no-kuni*) in fact means the Land of the Ripe Rice Ears. The first lesson in Japanese etiquette is to treat rice with veneration, and a man forgiven for squandering money will be condemned for wasting rice.

Rice means more to the Japanese than bread and potatoes combined mean to Americans. To Japanese rice is what reindeer are to the Lapps and the coconut palm is to natives of certain South Pacific islands. Rice provides them with food in variegated forms, drink (rice wine—sake), wearing apparel (sandals and rain-capes and rain-hats) of rice-straw, and elements of building materials (thatched roofs, matting, clay-and-straw mortar).

In Japan, rice is the very elixir of life. Ungarnished rice is relatively tasteless to us, but the Japanese savor and judge it with the same sensory concentration a native of France gives to wine tasting. For hundreds of years, taxes were paid in rice, and the wealth of the feudal lords was gauged by the number of *koku* (five bushels) of rice their fiefs produced. The rice harvest is accompanied and followed by religious rites, and the day when the Emperor pulls on his rubber boots and wades out in a wet rice paddy to plant the first rice shoot is a day of national significance. Even cats and dogs are fed rice.

Japanese insist on having at least two and often three rice meals daily. This devotion to the white grain, which is one hundred percent digestible, has doubtless saved the Japanese from many severe famines. An underlying principle of Japanese food consumption is to cram as much rice into the stomach as possible, and to make this unseasoned white manna somewhat more palatable, they take a nibble of vegetable, seasoned to provide a strong, counter-balancing taste, with every one or two large mouthfuls of rice. Many, however, eat rice with almost no side dishes. A favorite lunch, especially in hard times, is called *Hinomaru-bento*, or the Rising Sun lunch box. In the middle of a bed of plain white rice is placed one small red pickled plum. This plum is all that is eaten with the entire box of rice. The spot of red on the white rectangular background resembles the national flag, hence the name.

Rice and its cultivation have also contributed to certain national traits of the Japanese. The richer the grain, the proverb runs, the lower the rice plant bows its head. The heavier the head at the tip of the stalk, the farther it leans toward the earth. Thus, the more powerful the man, the more humble he becomes toward others, especially to inferiors.

The traditional Japanese virtues encompass self-effacement, humility and a willingness to yield to others. These traits are related to the desire to avoid confrontation and to achieve consensus (even occasionally at the cost of unresolved disagreements.)

These virtues and spiritual traits may have their origin in many centuries of the labor-intensive growing of rice that requires stable, smooth interpersonal relations. The very survival of entire farming communities required the close cooperation of all in watering and tilling small patches of arable land. Self-effacement was encouraged; self-assertion proscribed. The rights and feelings of the individual could not be allowed to compete with the welfare of the group.

Because they always insist that the hull and embryo bud be removed from their rice, the Japanese display a syndrome of troubles that point to a chronic deficiency of B complex vitamins. This results in ailments such as beriberi, nutritional edema, pellagra, keratitis, anemia, hindered secretion of hormones from the ovaries, and various disorders of the nervous system and brain. Because they must eat so much rice to feel satisfied and maintain strength, their stomachs become distended and so are positioned comparatively lower than in the West.

CONSIDERING THE POPULARITY of this rice dish in Japan and its spreading appeal in foreign parts, *sushi* deserves more than passing attention, although I must confess that despite a great many respectful pilgrimages to *sushi-ya* its attraction still escapes me.

A serviceable definition of *sushi* would be a two-bite oblong-shaped ball of lightly vinegared rice topped with a dab of a fiery, bilious-green horseradish called *wasabi* and a thin slice of raw fish or shellfish. It can also be made without fish. A hand-rolled shape is called *nigiri-zushi*, but it can be served in other forms.

Physically, most *sushi-ya* (*ya* means shop) are marvels of bright cleanliness. The white cypress woodwork is unpainted and scrubbed to crisply gleaming spotlessness daily. Well-placed, unobtrusive lighting chases shadows out the back door, and there are none of those smoky, grease-spattered, grime-encrusted nooks that worry the fastidious in greasy spoons I have entered elsewhere.

On the counter in front of the customer is a glassed-in case with a colorful array of varicolored crisply fresh marine exotica. The *sushi* master (called the *itamae*, or "in front of the board") and his helpers dress in clinically white smocks and caps or headbands and walk in high clogs. Three to five years of apprenticeship are required to become a competent *itamae*, who must be so deft in forming the *nigiri-zushi* with his left hand and two fingers of his right hand that it is said that all the grains of rice (between 300 and 350 in each piece of *nigiri-zushi*) run parallel with the length of these two oblong bites, not crosswise.

He must also be an early rising, knowledgeable shopper at the fish market. The freshness of the raw fish used in the best *sushi-ya* is so vital that the *itamae* recommends to his favored customers that they enjoy their sushi at noon rather than in the evening, the difference of five or six hours being important even to fish kept on ice.

How long the *itamae* will survive as a class is a moot question. The *sushi*-master's days may be numbered by the appearance on the scene of the *sushi* robot, developed after five years of research and capable of patting into shape about 1,200 oblong balls of vinegar-flavored rice an hour: three times the speed of the *itamae* with the fastest fingers. (Those fingers must still be used, however, to garnish the rice with *wasabi*—one bold step toward depravity—and then the *de rigueur* slice of raw fish, octopus, salmon eggs, or what have you.)

Even though these robots sell for $8,000 each, their demand is such that production can't keep pace with orders. For the most part, they are used in the back-room kitchens of fast-food and carry-out *sushi* shops, since the true *sushi* connoisseur will not countenance such cold-metal interference with traditional human skills.

Another aspect clouding the future of the *itamae* is the rising cost of ingredients, some of which have reached the ruinous stage, with resulting bad news to *sushi* devotees. The *sushi* epicure demands that his squid come from African waters, his sea urchin from southern California, his prawns from Mexico, and his giant bluefin tuna from the north Atlantic.

These tuna, which may cost as much as $13,000[*] each in Tokyo's Tsukiji fish market, are taken in the gelid waters of the Atlantic, chilled during their fifteen-hour flight to Tokyo, and, passing through several hands, are served to *sushi-ya* customers within five days of being caught.

The endangered bluefin may travel a long way before reaching the Tokyo diner's lips. Three-quarters muscle, the huge fish are capable of bursts of speed up to fifty-five miles per hour and can out-distance anything underwater except a killer whale and a mako shark. With their speed, they roam the far reaches of the North Atlantic, then—if caught for the Japanese market—are flown the eight thousand miles to Tokyo, and in some instances, proceed even farther to Southern California, ending up in one of the many *sushi-ya* in the Los Angeles area.

The Japanese have an obvious penchant for devising out-of-the-ordinary settings in which to dine on both the commonplace and the exotic. Perhaps this is a competitive necessary in a city like Tokyo that offers seventy styles of cooking in some thirty-five thousand restaurants. There are restaurants that serve only lobsters, others that serve only sardines. (One menu features sardine steak, consisting of ground sardines cooked like hamburger.) Or tortoise or crab or leech. Or *tofu*. Or horse meat, which the Japanese euphemistically call *sakura-niku* (cherry meat).

There are revolving restaurants and restaurants where the band goes up and down on an elevator-like stage. There are underground restaurants (many in the huge maze near Tokyo Station) and restaurants (*okonomi-yaki*) where you can cook food for yourself. Some restaurants

[*]In January 1997, a 389-pound bluefin tuna was sold at auction in Tokyo for $51,700. (Japan Airlines Newsletter)

are aboard barges on canals in downtown Tokyo and Osaka, some restaurants are perched above lonely coasts where the spray spatters the dining room windows when the sea is running. The restaurants connected to inns back in the hills serve only wild game—boar, deer, pheasant, and bear.

So much diversity is there that my memory boggles at retaining them all, but here are a few that stand out: in Tokyo you can rent an *ami-bune* (net-boat) that carries up to eight passengers—with perhaps a geisha or two—out into Tokyo Bay in the evening. Reaching a likely spot, the oarsman lets the boat, also called *a tempura-bune*, drift while he catches fish with a throw-net. While you drink beer or saké, he cooks the fish for you over a hibachi and serves them with rice and vegetables. And you can take home any leftover fish

A typical Japanese meal served at home.

One restaurant in the Ginza district of Tokyo has a fish tank next to the front door. You point out the fish that you want, and you can even net it yourself. The fish is taken to the kitchen where strips of raw flesh are sliced from its sides and served to you so quickly that you can still see some reflexive movements in the raw strips on the plate set before you. A restaurant in Mejiro in Tokyo, once the mansion of a wealthy family, has wooded park-like grounds where guests can eat outdoors during warm weather. Each summer the restaurant releases hundreds of thousands of fireflies on the premises, converting the grounds into a sea of stars.

The Kawajin Ryotei, an inn-like restaurant on the bank of the Edo River outside Tokyo, provides a bath—community-style for mixed bathing—for its diners, most of whom like to bathe before dinner. About forty minutes north of Tokyo, near the town of Urawa, stand several ancient farmhouses set on hillocks in a swampy region. This swamp provided Tokyo—or Edo—with eels during much of the Tokugawa Era. Now these two- and three-hundred-year old farmhouses have been converted to eel restaurants where customers can dine on generous portions of *unagi* while looking out over the swamp (where the eels are raised) and nearby woods.

I think the eatery that will remain most firmly fixed in my memory is a restaurant on the bank of a river near Tokyo where I went once to sample its tempura. As is customary, I took off my shoes at the entrance and was escorted to a *tatami* room with a low table at its center, *kotatsu* style, with an open pit under the table so diners can ease their legs by letting them dangle. In cold weather a hibachi is placed in the bottom of this space to warm the feet and legs of the guests. My visit was in August, though, and it was stifling hot. Even so, I could not understand why the waitress insisted that I remove my socks and roll up the legs of my trousers, although admittedly it felt good to place my hot, aching feet on the cool concrete at the bottom of the space under the table.

About the time my beer was served, I thought I felt a dampness around my feet and this sensation quickly grew until it became an undeniable flow of water. Puzzled but by no means displeased, I looked under the table, then asked for confirmation. The waitress told me the restaurant redirected a flow from the river to bathe the feet of guests in cool, running water throughout their meal.

## References

1.  Steinberg, Rafael. *The Cooking of Japan.* New York: Time-Life Books, 1969.

2.  Richie, Donald. *A Taste of Japan.* Tokyo: Kodansha International, 1985.

3.  Rifkin, Jeremy. *Beyond Beef.* New York: Penguin Books, 1992.

4.  Adams, Andy. "World-Famed Gourmet Says Kobe Beef Is Tops." *Japan Times* (Tokyo), July 2, 1961.

5.  Claiborne, Craig. "Where Unusual Restaurants Are Usual." *New York Times*, December 2, 1968.

6.  Adams, Andy. "Dissertation on Dining Off the Beaten Track." *Japan Times Weekly*, November 25, 1961.

7.  Kuroda, Kazuo. "Are We Eating Right?" *Japan Times*, March 1, 1958.

8.  Rabbitt, James A. *Rice in the Cultural Life of the Japanese People.* Tokyo: Asiatic Society of Japan, 1940.

## Chapter Nineteen

# An American Apostate Humanizes the Emperor

*Eleven months before Pearl Harbor, a missionary from Kansas chose to renounce his U.S. citizenship and throw in his lot with Japan. Yet in 1945, this man, so successful in many fields, approached Douglas MacArthur with an unusual proposal for smoothing the path of U.S.–Japan relations.*

### Omi on Lake Biwa 1905–1964

William Merrell Vories was born in Leavenworth, Kansas, on October 28, 1880. When he was six, he should have enrolled in the Leavenworth Public School, but the Vories family doctor would not permit him to attend school at all. That same day another lad Vories's age enrolled, perhaps sitting at the same desk Vories would have occupied.

The two boys never got to know each other in Kansas, and did not meet until fifty-nine years later in Tokyo. One of them now went by the name of Merrell Vories. The other was Douglas MacArthur.

More than a few Westerners have lived much of their lives in Japan, and some have had there remarkable, rewarding, and strange—by any measure—careers: Will Adams, Lafcadio Hearn, and William Willis being among them. But surely none of them stands taller on the scale of singularity than William Merrell Vories. The twists and turns in the path of his destiny, the impact he had on Japan, and his enviable romance with a loyal, handsome woman of the Japanese nobility make his story nothing if not extraordinary.

Growing up in Flagstaff, Arizona, Merrell—as he was usually called—was seldom in the best of health, but he was blessed with determination and ambition. He became an accomplished musician and (lesser) poet. Joining the YMCA, he began to have visions of doing the Lord's work in foreign lands.

William Merrell Vories, missionary and architect.
*Courtesy of John Hyde*

Having no visible opportunity to actually take the Gospel to alien parts, Vories knew he would need a work-a-day occupation and so chose architecture, for which he would prepare himself at Colorado College in Colorado Springs.

To support himself while there, he played the organ in a church and found a job as assistant secretary of the YMCA in Colorado Springs. After graduation, the Young Men's Christian Association offered to recommend him to a commercial high school in Omi-Hachiman, near Kyoto, Japan. The high school was seeking a teacher of English.

On a chilly February day in 1905, when Merrell was twenty-five years old, he stepped off the train at the Omi-Hachiman Station and looked around him at what he could see of this town of seven thousand heathens. He was separated from his heavy luggage at the port of Yokohama and was almost without money. The icy winds off Lake Biwa, Japan's largest inland body of water, pierced Vories' inadequate clothing. He spoke no Japanese. He was nine thousand miles from home. He was as homesick as he had ever been or was ever likely to be. (One of his few assets was his enchanting, joyous smile.)

Yet this was the town where he would spend the rest of his long, productive life, where he would design many of the town's buildings, establish a profitable business, and—above all else—where he would live with his one and only true love.

A brief history of that woman—Maki Hitotsuyanagi (the surname means "One Willow")—can hold its own with Merrell's. Maki was a petite (only five feet tall) Japanese of the noble class whose extant photos prove her to be extremely lovely. Her large dark eyes had the uncanny quality of seeming to penetrate to the very soul of anyone she gazed upon.

Maki's father, Viscount Suenori Hitotsuyanagi, had been *daimyo* of Iyo under the Tokugawa Shogunate and, although a difficult father for Maki to get along with, had been willing to raise his daughter in sumptuous surroundings. He spent much of his time trying to marry her to the scion of a rich, noble family, and she spent much of her time trying to thwart his plans (while studying English and the piano). Sadly, her mother had died when Maki was still very young, so the girl grew up lonely and unfulfilled.

Her brother Keizo had been adopted into the extremely wealthy Hiraoka family and had married that family's eldest daughter. With three small daughters, Keizo needed someone to superintend his nursery and so he asked his sister Maki to fill that role and she accepted with delight.

Her brother also continued efforts toward finding a suitable marriage partner for Maki while she grew ever more opposed to the idea of any arranged marriage or, because of what she had observed, of a Japanese husband.

At length, her despairing family hit on the idea of sending her to America, where she might find a husband among the overseas Japanese students. In this way, they reasoned, Maki could arrange her own marriage, perhaps with a Japanese who had absorbed enough of American ways not to be completely abhorrent to her.

She attended a preparatory school managed by Sophie and Abigail Kirke in Bryn Mawr, Pennsylvania, generally repeating the same courses that she had already taken back home in Japanese.

Deciding to become independent, Maki instructed her family in Japan to send her no more money. Upon completion of the preparatory school, a group of Philadelphia ladies offered her a scholarship to Bryn Mawr, which Maki gratefully accepted. Before finishing that college, however, she contracted typhoid fever, possibly from eating infected oysters. After a long spell of convalescence Maki was again without funds. She had no work and was not enrolled in school.

In the depths of Maki's gloom, an American woman, who coincidentally had taught her English in Japan, learned of her plight and asked Maki to come live with her. Alice Bacon lived in Deep Haven, Connecticut, with an English sheepdog named Grimmy. She was to become the mother Maki had so needed and longed for.

During the summers, Maki assisted her foster mother in managing a multiracial camp on Squam Lake in New Hampshire, wintering in Alice's New Haven home. This was a happy period in Maki's life.

But good things end. Maki received word from Japan that her father, the ex-*daimyo*, had not much longer to live and that she should hasten back to Japan. She did not want to leave her blissful home with Alice Bacon and Grimmy, but she had no choice.

Back in Japan, she made her father as comfortable as she could, then settled back to await the inevitable. But another sea change was about to occur in Maki's life style. Her brother Keizo, by now a successful businessman, told her he was discussing the construction of some new buildings with an American architect and to forestall possible linguistic problems, he wanted Maki to sit in on the conferences.

Maki and William Vories.
(Maki was the daughter of Viscount Hitotsuyanagi).

The architect turned out to be the blue-eyed, brown-haired Merrell Vories, the part-time missionary with the joyous smile. His smile alone, it was said, was enough to convert a heathen. He and Maki took one look at each other and knew instantly that something magical was about to take place. Both were smitten and fell quickly and completely in love with each other. He was thirty-nine and she thirty-five. Both Christians, they exchanged their vows in a Christian church (which he had designed). The bride wore white with a veil and the groom had donned a long frock coat and gray trousers. The year was 1919.

As the daughter of an ex-*daimyo*, Maki was registered with the Imperial Household and so had to obtain its permission to marry. This was not easy, for it was the first time in 2,000 years that one of the Household registrants was to be granted permission to wed a foreigner. When all was arranged, the newlyweds departed for a three-week honeymoon in the mountain resort of Karuizawa, northwest of the capital.

During the years since his arrival homesick and hungry in the lakeside town of Omi-Hachiman, Merrell Vories had not been lollygagging. While teaching English at the commercial middle school, he spent his otherwise free hours promoting missionary projects of many kinds. In fact, his intense enthusiasm for these projects and his unceasing advancement of Christianity in the classroom eventually lost him his teaching job. The school board recognized his excellence as a teacher, but the elders of the town wanted someone who would teach their children English—not the Gospel. They were, after all, Buddhists and Shintoists.

With more time to devote to his profession, architecture, Merrell established an office in Omi-Hachiman that eventually would be responsible for building nearly 1,600 churches, schools, hospitals (including the country's largest tuberculosis sanitarium), and residences all over Japan.

Vories founded his construction company on several unusual principles: more than half the profits were to be given over to the work of God; directors were not paid unless they actually worked in the company; commodities handled by the company were resold for only a modest profit that was added to the actual cost of acquisition; most important, no employee could work more than forty-four hours a week.

This last revolutionary provision shocked the construction industry in Japan. Not long thereafter, Vories and a competitor were engaged in constructing two similar buildings across the street from each other in bustling downtown Osaka. Vories's building proceeded at the pace demanded in his principles of incorporation—forty-four hours a week. The structure across the street followed the more feudalistic and longer standards. In the end, Vories's construction crew won the competition. Vories had been right: shorter hours gave his workers more energy and more enthusiasm.

If only there were a more thorough tabulation of all that Merrell got himself involved in during those years. Instead, there is a mention of him teaching English in one town, a Bible class in another. Buildings of his design were to be found here and there outside Japan, too, especially in Southeast Asia. The buildings themselves enhanced his architectural reputation for they were based on Vories's belief that the "dignity of a building is like a person's character—it lies less in its appearance than in its contents." Vories structures were esteemed as being neat, solid, reliable, and symmetrical. The town of Omi-Hachiman itself comprised so many of his structures that it was seen as a unique amalgam of East and West.

Vories's trips abroad in pursuit of God's work increased in frequency and after a time he found that he had crossed "the oceans" more than thirty times. Wherever he went, Vories was tireless in his proselytization and the acquisition of co-workers and supporters.

Another record reveals that Vories wrote the lyrics to the college song of Doshisha University in Kyoto—and that he designed the entire campus of the Kansei Gakuin (University) in Uegahara.

Once, at a Laymen's Missionary Convention in Chicago, he met a kindred soul—A.A. Hyde, president of the Mentholatum Corporation of Wichita, Kansas. The men were similar in that both agreed that all business should be carried on under the guidance of God. Their main difference was that Hyde had much more money.

At length, Hyde offered Vories an exclusive franchise to market his successful salve Mentholatum (Japan was the chief supplier of the main ingredient, menthol) if Vories would agree that a "great percentage of the profits would go to meet the spiritual needs of the Japanese."

Even if Hyde had not made that stipulation, Vories would have.

Hurrying back to Japan to devise a marketing program for Mentholatum, Vories was fortunate that his business and residence in Omi-Hachiman, had had a reputation for its population of merchants for four hundred years. In Japanese, in fact, it was called the *akindo no sato*, or "merchants' village."

In pursuit of business, Omi-Hachiman salesmen traveled on foot throughout Japan. They would carry kimono from Kyoto to Hokkaido and bring back dried fish. They were constantly on the alert for useful commercial information. These salesmen lent money to temples and shrines for restoration projects and other social undertakings, thereby gaining the trust and goodwill of the nearby people. From among these peregrinating merchants of Omi, Vories chose his first Mentholatum sales recruits.

Instead of kicking off his campaign with massive newspaper advertising, Vories chose to introduce Mentholatum by word-of-mouth, neighbor to neighbor. These "salesmen" passed along the message about the gentle efficacy of the salve.

Mentholatum was quickly on its way to national success in Japan. Most of the profits, in accord with Vories's agreement with A.A. Hyde, went into missionary work. Vories set up an a religious organization called the Omi Brotherhood. In fact, the Brotherhood was given the Mentholatum franchise and furthered its Christian undertakings with the proceeds from the franchise.

The business ran in that fashion for many years until it came under the control of the Rohto Pharmaceutical Co. of Japan, which also acquired the Mentholatum Co. of Wichita, Kansas, and its factory in Buffalo, New York.

In 1940 Vories began to hear ancestral voices prophesying war. It would be a day he had long dreaded. Yet, all the signs had been there for him to see. In 1925, when he had tried to take Maki with him on a trip to the United States, he was thwarted by the recent passage of the Oriental Exclusion Act by the U.S. Congress.

How should he respond? By now he had lived and thrived in Japan longer than he had ever lived in his native America. His home, his prospering business, the Christian purpose of his life were now all in Japan. Could he take Maki, who believed herself to be a citizen only of the Kingdom of God, with him wherever he went? If they went to America when war began, could or would they ever return to Japan? After all, his parents, who had come to live with him in Japan in their declining days, were buried in Omi-Hachiman. In fact, he had built a mausoleum for them carved into the stone face of a cliff, with niches designated for him and Maki.

At last Vories made up his mind: he would become a Japanese. But this was not to be—as Japanese were wont to say about anything easy to do—a "before-breakfast undertaking." In the years since the re-awakening of Japan to the West, few indeed had been those citizens of the "advanced nations" such as the United States and England who had elected to turn their coat and join one of the "less-advanced" nations.

After a considerable tussle with the authorities, Vories discovered that the best way (at least, it was the one he chose) to accomplish his conversion in nationality was to divorce his wife, renounce his U.S. status, apply for Japanese citizenship, take his wife's pre-marital surname of Hitosuyanagi, and be registered in the rolls of the Hitotsuyanagi clan, and endure seven months of other intricate formalities before he could become a Japanese—and remarry Maki. This he finally accomplished in January, 1941—eleven months before the attack on Pearl Harbor.

It would have been fascinating to have debated this decision with Vories. For all his intelligence, it is difficult to comprehend why he took this most important step. At the time, Vories declared three reasons for changing his nationality. First, he said, he had always disapproved of Europeans who had migrated to America without ever trying to become citizens. Second, he could see the "fairness of Japan's main position" and was determined to align himself in principle with his adopted country. Third, with Jesus Christ as his model, he wanted to be naturalized as a "human being" and not as a citizen of any particular nation.

Of the three reasons, the first was the only one that might be partially justified, although it was surely not his function to renounce his birthright merely to serve as an example to others. The second reason sounds like something Vories might have said to curry favor with the Japanese authorities. The third is pure hogwash.

Could there have been a more valid reason underlying Vories's camouflage? Perhaps. But Vories had made his decision and would have to lie in it.

Shortly before the opening of hostilities, Emperor Hirohito arranged a private, unofficial audience with Vories in the garden of the imperial palace in Kyoto. They spoke for nearly an hour, and the Emperor was reported to have been impressed with Vories' command of the Japanese language and his patriotism to his newly adopted country.

There seemed to be no doubt that Vories had become Japanese through and through. He had turned his coat and was now an apostate and beyond the pale.

Vories and his wife spent most of the war years in the mountain resort of Karuizawa, a refuge for many third-country nationals. With his considerable financial means, they must have suffered less than most Japanese, but it is doubtful that Vories and Maki escaped all the widespread tribulations so commonplace in wartime Japan.

On September 7, 1945, five days after the surrender ceremony on the USS *Missouri* in Tokyo Bay, Prime Minister Fumimaro Konoe asked Merrell Vories to visit Douglas MacArthur and sound out his intentions toward Japan in general and the Emperor in particular.

Two days later, Vories traveled along the war-torn roads to SCAP Headquarters, which was still in Yokohama. Knowing Vories to be a collaborator, MacArthur refused his request for an interview, saying that if Prime Minister Konoe wanted to speak to him he should come directly and not try communicating through an emissary.

Vories reported this rebuff to the prime minister, who then asked that Vories think of some reform that would catch MacArthur's eye and thus soften his heart toward the Emperor.

On the morning of September 12, Merrell Vories awakened in his room in the Imperial Hotel (undamaged by the B-29 raids) in Tokyo. He had a splendid idea, one that he believed was God sent: simply put, the Emperor of Japan should renounce his divinity.*

---

* In the United States, during the war, the desirability of a "renunciation of divinity" on the part of Japan's Emperor had been made several times by such Christian spokesmen as Willis Lamott. Vories may have been aware of these recommendations—or he may not.

Hirohito himself, like many educated Japanese, had never looked upon the occupant of the Peacock Throne as a god—at least not in the omnipresent, omnipotent Western sense. Instead, he regarded himself as a *kami*, or immortal spirit—a long way from being a "god."

Vories took his idea to the Prime Minister, who relayed it to Hirohito. Together they looked up "god" in a dictionary and there found the definition, among others, of "Master Craftsman of All Things." Hirohito did not believe he was the "Master Craftsman of All Things," so he agreed to announce that he was not.

MacArthur also approved, so this renouncement of divine status (*Ningen Sengen*) was incorporated into the Imperial radio message to the people of Japan on January 1, 1946. The Emperor's words, phrased though they were in an ancient form of Japanese, were a shocking revelation to the people.

Buried far down in the body of the message was the operative sentence: "The ties between Us and Our people have always stood on mutual trust and affection and are not predicated upon the false concept that the Emperor is divine and that the Japanese people are superior to other races and fated to rule the world. The Emperor is not a living god."

There it was. In flat unemotional words the Emperor told his people he was not a god. And that they, his subjects, were no better than anyone else. Try to imagine what shocking thoughts must have scorched millions of long-misled minds at that moment.

Apostate though he was, William Merrell Vories had done a good day's work. His idea would probably be of more benefit to his adopted country than all his 1,600 or so buildings and millions of jars of Mentholatum.

After the war Vories would have several meetings with grateful Hirohito as well as even one with Douglas MacArthur. Vories later told Maki that he had thanked the five-star general for giving back to Japan its self-respect, but the Supreme Commander for the Allied Powers waved aside gratitude, saying, "I am just trying to follow the Sermon on the Mount."

Vories was made the first honorary citizen of Omi-Hachiman in 1958—and he died in 1964. The lovely, faithful Maki died several years later, worshipping his memory to the end.

## References

1.     Fletcher, Grace Nies. *The Bridge of Love*. New York: Dutton and Co., 1967.

2.     Bergamini, David. *Japan's Imperial Conspiracy*. New York: William Morrow & Co., 1971.

3.     Vories, William Merrell. *The Omi Brotherhood in Japan*. Omi-Hachiman, Japan: The Omi Brotherhood Book Department, 1934.

4.     *Kodansha Encyclopedia of Japan*. Tokyo: Kodansha International Ltd., 1983.

5.     Irving, George. *Master of Money*. New York: Fleming H. Revel Co., 1936.

6.     Dower, John W. *Japan in War and Peace*. New York: The New Press, 1993.

## CHAPTER TWENTY

# The Supreme Hero of Modern Japan

*There was a childlike innocence about this mammoth man. Generous to a fault, he sometimes refused to accept his salary, protesting that he had not spent all the money from his previous pay period. As Japan's first field marshal, he commanded the army that restored Emperor Meiji to his throne, then rebelled against the Meiji oligarchy. Future generations of soldiers would revere him as the last true hero of Japan.*

## 1827-1877

The field marshal, a bullet lodged in his groin, knelt alongside the trail on the side of a hill in the southern city of Kagoshima. He pressed the tip of a short sword into the left side of his abdomen and slowly drew it across from left to right about an inch below his navel. (To have made the cut more quickly—with less pain—would have violated the soldier's samurai code of ethical behavior.) His jaw muscles knotted, the only visible sign of his suffering. His cheeks had just been rouged, for in death the face of a *hayato* (that is, a true Satsuma samurai) should retain its lifelike, ruddy complexion.

The field marshal nodded to his *kaishaku*, or assistant at *seppuku*, to proceed with the ritual. The assistant had been pouring water down the blade of his priceless Mitsutada sword so it would slice more easily through flesh. Seeing the nod, he rose to his feet and hefted the Mitsutada.

The date was September 24, 1877.

Would this be the final moment in the extraordinary life of Takamori Saigo—panegyrized by descriptions such as "supreme hero of modern Japan," the giant who strode his country as the Colossus straddled the Port of Rhodes?

Among many other qualities, Saigo was a fine poet, philosopher, compulsive letter writer, accomplished calligrapher (calligraphy being the supreme art of a Japanese gentleman), and scholar. While in exile for seven years on the islands south of his native Satsuma, Saigo read and digested all of the 1,200 books he had brought with him. (He also worked in the rice fields to help the downtrodden, half-starved peasants living near where he was loosely detained.) Like his father, who had been a sumo wrestler, the exiled Saigo honed his skills in the same "Sport of Elephants" with a noteworthy degree of success.

This man of commanding stature was worshipped as a god by some and called a superman by others. He was favorably compared with the Duke of Wellington — and to Abraham Lincoln.

He was an original whose like would probably never be seen again. Saigo's home was in Satsuma (now Kagoshima), the southernmost fiefdom on the island of Kyushu, where forty percent of the pugnacious population were samurai (the comparable figure for the rest of Japan was seven to ten percent), the remaining males wishing they could be.

Saigo proved a strangely gentle samurai, many of whose sayings were likened to those of Jesus Christ. The best known was *Aijin Keiten*, e.g., Revere Heaven, Love the People. He usually wore raggedy, thread-bare clothing, often going barefoot. He was distressingly honest, hating display and affectation, was modest to a fault, and so lacking in avarice that as a bureaucrat working in Tokyo, he sometimes went several months without drawing his salary. (When questioned, he explained he still had some money left over from his last pay so had no need for more in the meantime.)

Described as "one of the most splendid personalities in Japan's past," in his last few years Saigo was proscribed as a traitor by the Emperor Meiji—the same emperor Saigo had fought for to restore him to his Peacock Throne.

Today Takamori Saigo stands—remembered in bronze— at the entrance to Ueno Park in the north of Tokyo. The inscription on the huge statue reads:

> THE SERVICES FOR THE NATION PERFORMED BY OUR BELOVED TAKAMORI SAIGO REQUIRE NO PRAISE FROM OUR PEN, FOR THEY WERE ABUNDANTLY WITNESSED BY THE PEOPLE....

The legs of the statue are bronze pillars. Saigo's metal hands form massive, fearsome fists. There is almost no neck. (While alive the neck was 19 inches in diameter and the body weighed 240 pounds.) Saigo's huge brilliant eyes burned with demonic energy and strength of will. (His eyes were once described by the contemporaneous British diplomat Ernest Satow as "large black diamonds.") One of his childhood nicknames was *Omedama*, or Big Eye. (He was also called *Oudo*, or the Great Oaf.) Those eyes sparkled from under eyebrows bushy enough to be worthy of a fairy-tale ogre.

He had prodigious testicles, and at another time these were the source of much pain. In his final battle against the government, the *Seinan-no-eki* or Southwest Campaign, Saigo suffered from a hernia. Single-handed he had tried to lift a cannon and its carriage out of a ditch.) Saigo led his rebel force in a circuitous retreat around the island of Kyushu, marching in severe pain. At last, halfway around Kyushu, he had to carry his testicles in a basket hanging from a thong around his neck. Pretty soon, that method became inadequate and Saigo was transported in a palanquin.

He was a leader among those who worked for the restoration of the Emperor Meiji to the full authority of his throne. The de facto rulers of Japan—the Tokugawa shoguns—ever since the early 1600s had allowed the Western powers to knock down Japan's sacred portals and open the country to the West. Saigo resisted this development fiercely and led all the Imperial forces during the struggle to topple the Tokugawas.

SAIGO HAD NO INTEREST whatsoever in awards or honors, his disapproval extending to others who received them. A fellow cabinet member once received a bejeweled saber as a gift, of which he was inordinately proud. Somehow the "great Saigo" managed to have the weapon taken from him (exactly how is not explained), whereupon Saigo gave it to a cadet of his acquaintance.

Saigo's personal magnetism caused him to be liked and admired almost immediately upon acquaintance. This charisma was based in part on his powerful, monumental physique but just as much on his open, charming and radiant personality. With an earthy sense of humor, he laughed quickly and often and was blessed with a childlike enjoyment of life. Saigo was natural and direct with his equals and considerate and gentle toward those who were beneath him in the social scheme of Japan.

His first job was gardener on the estate of the *daimyo* of Satsuma, and after that he was bird keeper for the same *daimyo* at his mansion in Tokyo. These positions were hardly in keeping with Saigo's fate: war secretary of the Satsuma fief and the clan's chief emissary in Kyoto, where the Emperor still had his seat. Gradually, Saigo immersed himself in politics—he was wholly dedicated to the Emperor—and military affairs. He learned the latter art quickly and thoroughly, which was strange considering his innocent, childlike personality.

Despite the blandishments of the Western world, Saigo dug in his heels and remained profoundly Japanese, although he respected Western technology and knew Japan would have to acquire much of it if she were to survive.

To Saigo, "Westernization" translated into "corruption of the Japanese spirit." He was not without his supporters in this attitude, but many Japanese—especially important ones—were intent on aping foreigners,

imbibing willy-nilly of the Western cultural cup. Saigo resisted this sac-
rilege to the bitter end to such an extent that his spurning of Western
culture came to be regarded as old fashioned and even eccentric.

Statue of Takamori Saigo. Inscription reads: "The services that our beloved
Saigo Takamori rendered to the nation require no encomium, for they have
witnesses in the eyes and ears of the people..." *Courtesy of Kazutsugu Araki*

Although Saigo objected to what he termed the "corruption" of public
officials, he supported centralization of the government in Tokyo. In
1873, while several leading government officials were traveling abroad

on the "Iwakura Mission," Japan received an official letter from the nation of Korea that read in part: "the western barbarians are beasts. The above we intend as a direct insult to you and your allies, the barbarians... .for either Japan must invade Korea, or Korea will invade Japan."

Taking advantage of the absence of other ministers (Saigo was a state counselor), he decided to lead an expedition across the Sea of Japan to punish the "arrogant Koreans."

The Iwakura Mission got back to Japan just in time to head off the expedition, but that was the beginning of Saigo's disenchantment with the administration and the hardening of his resolve to revive Japan's previous feudalistic state. Supporting him were many idle samurai who had cheered the idea of a punitive expedition to Korea, since, among other things, it would have given them employment again.

So Saigo the Great resigned from the government and retired to his home in Satsuma.

During his years of retirement, Saigo mostly occupied himself with the establishment of a military academy, which with its branches eventually boasted a cadet student body of twenty thousand. The government in Tokyo regarded Saigo's military schools as hotbeds of rebellion, which, of course, is pretty much what they were.

About this time a series of violent revolts began to break out in Japan, especially in the southwest. The rebels were mostly malcontent samurai who resented the loss of their topknots and their privilege to carry two swords, the loss of emoluments from their former *daimyo* as well as the large-scale introduction of Western culture. The leaders of these uprisings tried to persuade Saigo to take command of their forces, but he adamantly refused.

However, the Tokyo government suspected that Satsuma, Saigo's fief, stood behind these mutinies and began dispatching informants to Satsuma, especially into Saigo's military academies. This tactic enraged Saigo and stimulated the onset of his rebellion: the so-called Southwest Campaign.

Forming an army of cadets from among his academies and from disenchanted samurai, the Great Saigo marched north to Kumamoto, where he laid siege for fifty-five days to the government castle in that city. When his force failed to capture it, Saigo began a circular retreat around Kyushu, the Kangun (government army) hot on his trail.

Statue of Takamori Saigo.

After walking—or being carried—298 miles in 18 days, Saigo closed the circle and re-entered his point of origin (and home), Kagoshima, where he was surprised and delighted to find no enemy troops. With 400 rebels still under his command, Saigo fortified a hill called Shiroyama, 350 feet high. The forces settled down to await the inevitable confrontation.

The ensuing siege lasted three weeks, the vastly superior government force surrounding the hill, leaving no chance for escape. In fact, it seems likely that Takamori Saigo had no real wish to escape and meant to die where he stood.

Rebel supplies, ammunition and able-bodied men were diminished day by day.

When Saigo was hit in the groin by an enemy bullet, he fell to the ground and said to one of his most faithful followers, Shinsuke Beppu, "We might as well do it here, don't you think?"

After making the obligatory slash across his abdomen, the "most potent personality in the history of Japan" signaled he was ready to be separated from his head. Beppu, elected to serve as executioner, botched the first swing of his blade and cut his leader's massive neck only halfway through. After one more cut, though, Saigo's head was severed, rolling off the trail into a ravine. One of Saigo's rebel samurai slid down to retrieve the massive head, then hid it in the brush about forty yards from where the others were waiting.

Surviving eyewitnesses wrote that more than one hundred samurai were visible up and down the trail, above and below Saigo's headless corpse. They had been standing stiffly erect and waiting silently. Almost in unison these samurai squatted along the path and bared their rear ends. It may have looked as if they were going to engage in a ritual of simultaneous defecation, but their intent was merely to stuff cotton into their rectums. The code of Bushido demanded they prevent themselves from evacuating their bowels when their sphincter muscles relaxed after death... thereby offending the olfactory sensibilities of anyone approaching their corpses.

That done, they applied rouge and a lip-reddening salve to one another's faces, then paired off to commit *seppuku* and be decapitated by their partners. The number of pairs kept dwindling until only one or two remained.

When government soldiers occupied Shiroyama, their primary assignment was to find Saigo, his body or his head. At length they located the latter and lovingly washed it, then brought it to be inspected by General Yamagata, commander of government troops. Holding the head respectfully, Yamagata bowed to it and said, "Ah, what a gentle look you have on your face."

Another suggestion of the affection with which Saigo was regarded even by his enemies was that the squad of soldiers that shot Saigo in the groin broke down crying when congratulated on their marksmanship.

## References

1. Mounsey, Augustus H. The Satsuma Rebellion. London: John Murray, 1879.

2. Morris, Ivan. The Nobility of Failure. Tokyo and Rutland, Vt.: Charles E. Tuttle Co., 1975

3. Tanaka Sogoro. Saigo Takamori. Tokyo: 1950.

4. Nishida Kazuo. "Guns and Christ in Kagoshima." Asia Scene (Tokyo), January 1965.

5. Bergamini, David. Japan's Imperial Conspiracy. New York: William Morrow & Co., 1971.

## CHAPTER TWENTY-ONE

# The First American Teacher of English in Japan

*Part Chinook Indian, part Scot, he was slender, bookish and very curious. He knew Japan was forbidden territory, but sneaked in anyway...and ended up in prison, from where he taught English to the future leaders of Japan.*

In 1848 one of the strangest foreigners from Japan's past stole ashore on an isolated coast. Considering the fate that might well have befallen him, this man's stealthy intrusion into the empire of the Shogun was an act of almost unimaginable courage. Ranald MacDonald (1824–1894), was the son of a Scottish trader and a Chinook Indian princess. Awaiting most foreign "barbarians" who knocked at Japan's portals without proper invitation were occasional lengthy terms of imprisonment and sometimes even decapitation.

What saved twenty-four-year-old Ranald from such treatment was carried in the seaman's bag he had slung over one shoulder. In those times most foreign sailors landing on the prohibited beaches of Japan would have carried with them, if anything, tobacco, hardtack, rum, and whiskey. But when he dropped it to the ground, young Ranald's bag neither clinked or clattered. It landed instead with a soft thud.

In appearance, MacDonald was slight and slim and at the time without the beard he grew later in life. His eyes were dark, as was his hair, and he wore the jacket and pants typical of whalers in the mid-nineteenth century. Except for its contents, his seaman's bag was not unusual. Nothing strange about any of that, but what was odd about this uninvited visitor was his reason for coming to Japan, which was curiosity, pure and simple. There had been many motivations for other unwelcome intrusions by the other foreign mariners: the desire to trade, a need for supplies, maritime emergencies, sometimes the desire to carouse ashore and pursue heathen women, and even a need for navigational charting, but MacDonald may have been—and perhaps likely was—the only man who came to Japan to satisfy his curiosity.

Born February 3, 1824, in Fort George in what was then the Oregon Territory (Oregon became part of the United States in 1845, so this young man was an American citizen from then on), his mother was daughter of the chief of the Chinook Indian tribe. The chief's name was Com-Comly. So extensive was his influence in that region he was called "King of the Columbia" and his daughter, the "Princess Sunday."

This dusky belle caught the roving eye of Archibald MacDonald, a trader from Scotland who came to Oregon Territory for the fur-trading Hudson's Bay Company. He may have had royal blood in his veins too, for he was of the Ranald Clan of Scotland, which had produced several Scottish kings.

Not long after their baby was born, Princess Sunday died. Ranald was adopted by the family of Chief Com-Comly, where he learned to speak the Chinook tongue before learning any English.

After a time, Archibald MacDonald remarried and moved with his bride and son to what is Portland , Oregon, where Ranald entered school. He was said to "consume textbooks faster than they could be assigned." One day in the 1830s, three visitors came to the district where the MacDonalds lived. So unusual were they that they sparked a fiery curiosity in the boy's curious mind.

The background of the three visitors is a story in itself. On October 11, 1832, the fishing boat *Hojun-maru* set sail from Toba (near present-day Nagoya) with fourteen hands. It was bound for Edo (now Tokyo) but an irate storm intercepted and demasted the *Hojun-maru*, blowing the small vessel far off course.

For fourteen months the fishing boat without sails and powerless to change direction, drifted slowly eastward across the vast North Pacific. Starvation combined with the elements to kill the crew one by one. By the time the *Hojun-maru* reached shore at Cape Flattery in what is now the state of Washington, only three sailors remained alive—Kyukichi, Otokichi, and Iwakichi.

The three Japanese were taken in hand by Indians somewhat less civilized than the Chinooks and kept as slaves until a British ship found them and reported their location to the Hudson's Bay Company. The fur traders, thinking they might somehow utilize these Japanese to drive a wedge into Japan's closed doors, bargained for their release and sent them to school to learn English, prior to returning them to Japan

Ranald MacDonald had heard a great deal about these three sea-waifs, and wondered if the Japanese might be related to his mother's Chinooks. Indeed, a surviving photo of Ranald, though dim, does reveal a faintly Oriental physiognomy.

In 1838, when Ranald was fourteen, his father sent him to a four-year school of higher learning in Canada. After completing his studies with excellent marks, the young man went to work in a bank in St. Thomas, Canada. But Ranald's destiny was not in banking. Later, he wrote that he "hated banking" and he yearned mightily to roam the world and quench his thirst for knowledge about other people and their cultures, especially the people of mystery-shrouded feudal Japan.

But Japan was still in its closed country period (*sakoku jidai*). Other than a few Dutch and Chinese, no foreigners were ever allowed to enter Japan for any reason and those attempting to do so could be and some-times were punished by death.

Regretfully postponing his visit to Japan, Ranald MacDonald quit the bank and went east to the Mississippi, where he hired on a steam-boat. Next on ocean-going vessels, he fulfilled his dream of roaming the seas for five years. Once the currents carried him to the whaling grounds off northern Japan and though he did not land, his ship came close enough that the crew could easily see beacon fires burning on hill-tops signaling the approach of a detested foreign vessel. They also sight-ed several *torii,* the obligatory archways before Shinto shrines. (Whalers on the western rim of the Pacific commonly believed the myth that those archways stood there solely for the purpose of hang-ing alien intruders.)

Ranald MacDonald, English teacher and adventurer.
*Courtesy of Eastern State Historical Society, Spokane (L94-11.28)*

In 1847, in Hawaii, MacDonald, seaman's bag on his back, trudged up the gangplank of the American whaler *Plymouth.* The captain had told young Ranald it was his intent to hunt whales in the Sea of Japan. MacDonald determined to leave the *Plymouth* off the coast of northern Japan, working as a deck hand until that opportunity materialized.

In his bag Ranald packed a Christian Bible, a book of prayers, a dictionary, and books on grammar, history and geography. In a small rowboat, he left the comparative comfort of the whaler on June 27, 1848, to the regretful farewells of his shipmates, who had found him decent, inoffensive, and much smarter than they. Through rough seas, Ranald MacDonald rowed to the island of Yagishiri, where at length he was found by two Ainu men.

The Japanese authorities also heard about Ranald and sent a perplexed message to the Shogun in Edo asking what they should do about this intruder. While they waited for an answer, MacDonald, according to his later autobiography, was treated with kindness. It was obvious, he wrote, that the Japanese found him just as curious a creature as he did them. Besides, his seaman's bag of books made a favorable impression, since other foreign seafarers were more likely to have bags filled with precious bottles.

The Shogunate decided Ranald should be sent from Ezo (Hokkaido) to Nagasaki, far to the southwest. There Ranald was held captive in a small room in a temple called the Daihian. A guard stood outside his door at all times.

This son of an Indian princess remained in the Nagasaki temple from October till the following April. During those winter months, he befriended an interpreter named Einosuke Moriyama, who, Ranald said, was intelligent and spoke "pretty good" English. Besides Moriyama, many other Japanese visited: officials, samurai, students, and priests.

Almost every day at least fourteen men came to the Daihian to learn English. After the Meiji Restoration of 1868, some of them became government leaders.

Ranald MacDonald spent his seven months in Nagasaki teaching. One day in the last month, he heard the sound of cannon: guns warning of the approach of a foreign ship, this the U.S. man-of-war *Preble*. The captain was a Commander Glynn.

Commander Glynn had entered the harbor of Nagasaki and sent a letter ashore to the local magistrate, who knew nothing of the rankings and titles of Americans. The magistrate sent for Ranald and asked for an explanation.

MacDonald began at the top with the "people," then the president, the vice-president, and all the way down to the naval rank of commander. The magistrate was puzzled. How could the "people" stand above the president or a king?

MacDonald's last act as a teacher in Japan was to explain that the United States was a democracy. "The people *are* king. They are the source of all authority."

He was taken away from Japan aboard the *Preble* on April 26, 1849. Leaving this man-of-war in Hong Kong, he set sail for Singapore and then for Australia, where he made a good deal of money in the gold fields.

With his money the son of Archibald MacDonald continued his foreign travels, returning at last to British Columbia in 1853. For the next three decades, he worked at various trades. In 1885 he settled in Fort Colville, Washington, where he lived as a hermit in a lonely cabin with only a dog as his companion. During this time he worked on his autobiography, although he did not live to finish it.

In his book Ranald wrote, "I have never ceased to feel most kindly and ever grateful to my fellow men of Japan for their really generous treatment of me. [I have] come across many people. . .but there are none whom I esteem more highly than my old hosts of Japan."

Had this been the autobiography of one of the more ordinary run of foreign tars—some victims of Japanese harshness and aloofness—how different his opinion of the Japanese might have been.

This son of an Indian princess and a Scottish clansman died August 5, 1894. The final words of the "first American teacher of English in Japan" were spoken to his niece, in whose arms he expired. (His canine companion stood guard by the bedside eyeing with suspicion all who approached his master.) The niece did not quite understand all his last words, but it was later explained to her that he had said, "*Sayonara,* my dear, *sayonara.*"

His body was interred in an old Indian cemetery—in an unmarked grave.

## References

1.  Williams, Harold S. *Foreigners in Mikadoland.* Tokyo:  Charles E. Tuttle Co., 1963.

2.  Plummer, Katherine. *Ranald MacDonald, the First Foreign English Teacher in Japan.* Tokyo: Tokyo YWCA, 1982.

3.  Seward, Jack. *Human Bridges between Japan and the West.* Tokyo: New Currents International Co., 1994.

4.  Lewis, William S., and Murakami Naojiro, eds. *Ranald MacDonald—The Narrative of His Early Life on the Columbia Under the Hudson's Bay Company's Regime; Of His Great Adventure to Japan; With a Sketch of His Later Life on the Western Frontier 1824-1894.* Spokane, Washington: Eastern Washington State Historical Society, 1923.

5.  Nicols, Marie L. *Ranald MacDonald, Adventurer.* Caldwell, Idaho: Caxton Printers Ltd., 1940.

## CHAPTER TWENTY-TWO

# Deadly Metal into the Abdomen

⟨⟨≈⟩⟩

*Several are the ways by which we can arrange our own exit from this vale of tears but cutting open the abdomen is not one of the preferred methods. At least, not in America.*

Of all the Japanese customs, perhaps none is stranger in Western eyes than self-disembowelment (*seppuku* or hara-kiri).

During the Sengoku Era of Japanese history (1467–1568), the commander of one of Lord Mori's castles, Muneharu Shimizu, was ordered to eviscerate himself. On the evening of the hara-kiri ceremony, a loyal vassal of Shimizu's—a man named Shirai—sent a message to his master begging that he deign to come to Shirai's room. Although understandably preoccupied with thoughts about and preparations for his departure from this world, which was to take place in less than an hour, Shimizu took the time to go to his favorite vassal's quarters in a far corner of the castle.

When Lord Shimizu arrived, Shirai was sitting with his legs crossed on the matting. Humbly he asked his master to sit down beside him, whereupon he began to tell Shimizu that he should not fear death, that he should approach it with courage and equanimity, and that self-disembowelment was not, after all, such a fearful demise.

Shirai coughed once and swayed slightly, then he opened his robe.

"You see, sire," he said, exposing the bloody slash across his abdomen, "I committed hara-kiri myself as soon as I was sure you were coming here. I wanted to show you that this is not so difficult a thing to do after all."

Overcome with gratitude, Shimizu rose to his feet beside his faithful retainer and unsheathed his long sword. With tears in his eyes, he raised his blade and with it sliced off Shirai's head, thereby performing the act of *kaishaku* and according to his old friend and vassal high honor.

After a few minutes of silent grief, he cleaned his sword, then walked back to meet his own end with renewed courage.

A similar but little-known incident took place in 1944 in Cowra, Australia, when the Japanese inmates of a prisoner-of-war camp broke out of captivity and fled into the Australian countryside one night in August. When the Australian guards entered the prisoners' barracks after the break, they found the bodies of eleven Japanese hanging from roof-beams. Interrogation of prisoners recaptured later revealed that those eleven men had been the instigators of the escape and that they had hanged themselves in front of all the other prisoners to demonstrate their own willingness to die and to give their comrades courage.

These two illustrations should suggest that the Japanese institution of suicide is a remarkable, if not unique, phenomenon in the annals of mankind's reasons for and methods of self-destruction. Although Westerners perhaps think of hara-kiri first in connection with Japanese suicides, the earliest recorded cases in Japan were accomplished by hanging and self-incendiarization, the usual manner of the latter being for the victim to set fire to his own home with himself inside.

Yoshiteru Murakami, a warrior of Japan's feudal days, managed to combine both self-incendiarization and hara-kiri in his own dramatic demise, when he and his master, Prince Morinaga, were trapped in a house by their enemies. Wanting to distract the foe so that his master could escape, Murakami climbed to the roof with a torch in his hand. With it, he set fire to the thatch, which blazed up brightly while Murakami yelled taunts to the enemy samurai below in the garden.

"Dogs!" Murakami shouted, "I am Prince Morinaga. Watch! I'll show you cowards how a true warrior dies."

In the light of the leaping flames from the thatched roof, Murakami glanced back and saw the dim form of Prince Morinaga disappear over the garden wall at the back side of the house. Reassured, he turned back to the now intently watching foe clustered below him.

Woodblock print that depicts some of the forty-seven Ronin preparing to invade the Edo mansion of Lord Kira to find Lord Asano, whom they blame for the death of their master. (Utagawa Kuniyoshi) Kuniyoshi, Japanese, 1798-1861, The Night Attack, Act I of the Chushingura, ink and color on paper, early 1830s, Kate S. Buckingham Purchase Fund, 1976.108; photograph © 1996, *The Art Institute of Chicago, all rights reserved*

Without another word, Murakami shed his outer robe and withdrew his dagger. With great resolve, he made a long, deep slash across his abdomen, just below the navel. Despite the excruciating pain and the blinding heat from the flames, he kept his body straight and his face impassive as his intestines came cascading through the cut. Seizing a slimy handful with his left hand, he cut them loose with the dagger in his right.

Tossing the dagger aside, he threw the ropy intestines down into the faces of his startled enemies. Then with one final effort he unsheathed his sword, inserted the point in his mouth, and fell forward on it and into the flaming thatch.

This was one of the early instances of hara-kiri or *seppuku* (both mean stomach-cutting) in Japanese history and took place long before it had become a formalized ceremony, encumbered with almost as many traditions and rules as the coronation of a monarch.

*Seppuku* became popular among the Japanese as a means of ending one's life partly because the abdomen was regarded as the seat of all emotions, the abode of the soul. Their language has many expressions that support this: *Hara ga tatsu* (the abdomen stands up) means to get angry. *Hara-guroi hito* (a man with a black abdomen) means a sly, cunning man. *Hara wo kimeru* (to decide the abdomen) is the equivalent of to make up one's mind. *Kare no hara ga yomenai* (I cannot read his abdomen) is similar to saying I cannot understand what's in his mind.

One little understood aspect of formalized *seppuku* is that the stomach cut alone was usually not fatal. This incision was made from left to right just below the navel but was not deep. The above-quoted cases in which the intestines poured out through the wound were exceptional and took place before *seppuku* became a ritualized method of punishment. Some men, in fact, barely scratched their skins with the tips of their daggers.

Once incision was made, the kneeling man signaled, by nodding his head or raising a finger for his assistant, who was poised to his left rear, to chop off his head. The role of this assistant, or *kaishaku*, also became formalized and required great skill. Some *kaishaku* could lop off a head and leave it hanging from the trunk of the body by a shred of skin. To cut the head off entirely was considered poor form, since it was liable to roll around and perhaps even spatter distinguished witnesses with blood.

In 1603 a long period of internal chaos and warfare in Japan ended with the commencement of the Pax Tokugawa: two hundred and sixty-five years of peace under the strict, far-sighted master administrators of the

Tokugawa clan. But these same years brought bitter disappointment to many samurai who could no longer "die in the presence of the master's horse."

In order to prove their courage, the samurai now had to contrive other excuses for self-immolation. The slightest embarrassment before superiors or a peccadillo in court etiquette could become the primer for triggering hara-kiri. The death of a *daimyo* would have the samurai standing in line, hara-kiri knife ready in hand, eager to follow the master in death.

The Tokugawas scented the danger inherent in unrestricted self-disembowelment and expressed their disapproval in various ways during the initial years of the Pax.

The warriors, however, still labored under the hypnosis of a death wish. In the words of Edwin Baelz, a German scholar and teacher of medicine at the Imperial University in Tokyo, "The life and education of the samurai was nothing more than preparation for a noble death."

Finally in 1682, the Tokugawa dynast put his formal stamp of disapproval on *seppuku*, expressing it in the form of a stern shogunal edict. He warned that families of the abdomen-cutters would be beheaded.

But there was a loophole: hara-kiri could still be ordained as an official punishment. Such punishment could be meted out not only by the Tokugawa government but by any of the clan chiefs of Japan. At the time of the hara-kiri prohibition, there were two hundred and twenty-nine feudatories—small and large—in Japan, and all of these, together with a considerable number of Tokugawa officials, were empowered to mete out the sentence dictating deadly metal into the abdomen.

(It should be pointed out that most samurai did not regard the sentence of hara-kiri as a punishment. Their first reaction was usually to thank the sentencing official for the "privilege" of being permitted to perform hara-kiri.)

It was about twenty years after the Tokugawa interdiction that the most famous real-life drama involving hara-kiri in Japanese history took place. A play based on these happenings is still performed annually in

Japan, on the anniversary of the event, and it draws mighty throngs who come to thrill, weep, and cheer.

This was the *Chushingura*: the story of the forty-seven ronin, called the Revenge of the Loyal League or the Treasury of Loyal Retainers. The three protagonists were Lord Kira, Lord Asano, and Oishi, a samurai retainer of Lord Asano.

Lord Asano, believing himself to have been insulted by Lord Kira, made the fatal mistake of drawing his sword in the Shogun's palace (a serious crime) in Edo and inflicting two slight wounds on Kira. Accordingly, the Shogun sentenced the unrepentant Lord Asano to commit hara-kiri, which he did in the late afternoon of the same day.

(Contrary to popular belief in Japan, Lord Asano did not actually cut his stomach open. In the confusion of the happenings of the day, Asano's hara-kiri knife had been taken away from him by the Shogun's palace guards and could not be found when the sentence was about to be hurriedly carried out. Asano had been taken to the residence of another *daimyo* who agreed to lend Asano a fine old hara-kiri blade that was a family heirloom. The assisting *kaishaku*, however, was a retainer of this *daimyo* and hated to see his master's heirloom besmirched by the blood of the wretch Asano, whom he despised. Therefore, he hastened to cut off Asano's head before Asano could plunge the heirloom into his intestines.)

The retainers of Lord Asano were enraged at Lord Kira for his insult to their lord and its dire consequence and vowed vengeance. This, however, was expected of them—vendettas being something of a national sport—and they were placed under the surveillance of the *metsuke*—the Shogun's watchdogs.

To allay suspicions, the Asano retainers, led by Oishi, launched themselves—they were now *ronin*, or masterless samurai—on a calculated, lengthy bacchanalia. Oishi himself moved to Kyoto where he deliberately drank himself into a stupor and slept in the gutter night after night. He also abandoned his wife, two of his younger children, and his aged father in order to lull Lord Kira and the Shogunal spies into believing that no mischief could come from such a besotted derelict.

Eventually, after many adventures and tribulations forty-seven of Asano's ex-retainers gathered in Edo at Oishi's behest. It was December 14, 1702. The very date strengthened the hearts—or stomachs—of these men because it was the anniversary of the death of their beloved Lord Asano.

In the chill of a snowy night, they surrounded, then invaded Kira's mansion. Kira was finally discovered cowering in a charcoal shed. He was decapitated on the spot. The assassins then filed through the dark streets of Edo to the Sengakuji Temple in Shinagawa and placed Lord Kira's carefully washed head on the gravestone of their beloved Lord Asano.

Having prohibited vendettas as well as unauthorized hara-kiri, the Shogun had no choice but to mete out condign punishment to Oishi and his men, although public as well as much official sentiment favored the vengeful retainers. He ordered that they be permitted to commit hara-kiri.

It was questionable that their rank as masterless samurai even entitled the group to the honorable sentence of hara-kiri, but the ceremony itself was carried out with all the pomp and elegance due a *daimyo* of the highest rank. Perhaps, for once, the Shogun attained his so sublime object by letting the punishment fit the crime.

The official who pronounced the sentence of death expressed his keen sympathy for the cause of the Asano retainers and endeavored to cheer them by announcing that the Shogun had abolished Lord Kira's feudal domain and that the surviving members of the lord's family had been dispossessed of all they owned and banished from the capital.

Whereupon the loyal retainers, still led by Oishi, mounted a platform one by one and without hesitation or sign of nervousness performed hara-kiri. By then, their number had been reduced to forty-six. Oishi had sent one man by the name of Terazaka to inform Lord Asano's widow of the heart-warming news. Terazaka's absence from the ritual branded him a coward in the public eye, but he later appeared before the Shogun and requested that he too be permitted to commit hara-kiri in like manner.

Strangely, the Shogun secretly gave him some money and told him to make himself scarce for a while. Terazaka later returned to the capital and lived there till his death at the age of eighty-two.

Two of Japan's most famous *daimyo*, Nobunaga Oda (1534–82) and Kenshin Uesugi (1530–78), were the bitterest of rivals. With unwavering and malevolent determination, both continually hatched assassination plots against each other.

They each employed full detachments of *ninjutsu-zukai* (*ninja*, or "men of stealth") to probe the other's weaknesses and to devise stratagems and subterfuges to bring about the other's downfall by surprise, cunning, or treachery.

These silent, dark-draped agents of stealth, the *ninjutsu-zukai*, or *suppa*, conducted their covert warfare at night while others slept. Few knew their faces, but their skills, endurance, and ingenuity were awesome.

If Oda's men bested their foes in one such undercover engagement, Uesugi's camp would emerge victorious in the next. The hostile tides ebbed back and forth, with the principals, Oda and Uesugi, surviving unscathed at the center of the strife and bloodshed.

In one intrusion into Uesugi's castle, three of Oda's *ninja* were slain. While chortling over this minor triumph, Uesugi permitted the relaxation of his defenses for a mite too long.

During that brief space of time, a certain Jinnai Ukifune—an Oda adherent—breached the castle's security and crept into the private quarters of Kenshin Uesugi, where the *daimyo*'s private toilet was to be found.

Jinnai Ukifune's principal distinction was his height: barely three feet tall. For this mission he had accustomed himself to living for days on end in earthenware jars that looked too small even to hold a tiny man's body.

The flooring of Uesugi's toilet was made of tile with a slitted opening in the center over which the user squatted while his wastes dropped into a narrow metal tank directly underneath the ten-inch-wide slit.

This tank was three-and-a-half feet in depth, and the fecal matter therein was often allowed to rise to well over the halfway mark and was seldom emptied. The stench was throat-grabbing and reputedly capable of asphyxiating cockroaches.

Oda's dwarf agent surreptitiously entered the toilet, squeezed his body—and his short spear—down through the ten-inch slit. He sank below the surface of the excreta in the tank, breathing through a hollow tube, the end of which protruded a scant two or three inches above the scummy surface.

As Jinnai knew he would sooner or later, Kenshin Uesugi returned to his quarters and squatted over the evacuation slit late that evening, the moment Jinnai had been waiting for.

Quietly he half stood in the excrement and wiped his eyes clear. Then he wiped clean the shaft of his short spear so that his hands could maintain a firm purchase. Raising the point of the spear to where it almost touched the *daimyo*'s fully exposed anus, the dwarf braced himself and thrust his weapon with all his strength precisely through the anal opening.

Which must have come as a surprise to Lord Kenshin Uesugi. He staggered out of his toilet and collapsed on the resilient matting of his large central room. His spear-pierced heart had stopped before the first of his retainers reached his side.

The dwarf sank back into the liquid manure. He was never discovered by any of Uesugi's warriors, who, shouting wild alarms, scampered about searching for the assailant.

The following night Jinnai made his escape through a crenel and down the castle wall, gratefully submerging himself in the relatively clean water of the moat. He cleaned himself as well as he could, then swam across the moat and made his escape.

Uesugi's survivors did not make public the true circumstances of his death, which, if known, it would certainly have made their *daimyo* the brunt of bawdy derision for many years.

## References

1.  Draeger, Donn F. *The Art of Invisibility: Ninjutsu*. Tokyo: Simpson-Doyle & Co., 1971.

2.  Seward, Jack. *Hara-Kiri: Japanese Ritual Suicide*. Tokyo: Charles E. Tuttle Co., 1968.

3.  Murdoch, James. *A History of Japan*. London: Routledge & Kegan Paul, Ltd., 1949.

4.  Shioya Sakae. *Chushingura, An Exposition*. Tokyo: Kenkyusha, 1940.

5.  Nitobe Inazo. *Bushido, The Soul of Japan*. Tokyo: Shokabo, 1900.

6.  Lord Redesdale. *Tales of Old Japan*. Tokyo: Charles E. Tuttle Co., 1966.

7.  Wada Katsunori. *Seppuku Tetsugaku* (Philosophy of *Seppuku*). Tokyo: Shubunsha, 1927.

8.  Baelz, Erwin. *Baelz Diary*. Tokyo: Iwanami Bunko Co.

9.  Storry, Richard. *The Way of the Samurai*. New York: Galley Press, 1978.

## CHAPTER TWENTY-THREE

# Japan Tests an Atom Bomb

*Anti-American voices in Japan have long fulminated against Americans for heartlessly and needlessly dropping two atomic weapons on Hiroshima and Nagasaki. But that same week the Japanese tested their own atom bomb with every intention of using such an explosive against the Allied invasion fleet off the coast of Kyushu in the fall of 1945.*

RADIO NEWSCASTERS everywhere must have grown hoarse as they excitedly narrated the events that shook the world during the week beginning August 6, 1945. And they might have lost their voices entirely had they learned that in the midst of all this, on August 11, 1945, Japan had test-fired its own atomic weapon on an island off the coast of Korea.

On August 6, the U.S. dropped an atom bomb—affectionately dubbed "Little Boy"—on Hiroshima, Japan.

Quick to grasp the opportunity, Joseph Stalin declared the Soviet Union to be at war with Japan on August 8.

On August 9, a B-29 called "Bock's Car" unloaded a plutonium bomb with the nickname "Fat Man" on Nagasaki. ("Fat Man" missed its aiming point by two miles, thereby saving several tens of thousands of lives.) On August 14, Air Force General Curtis LeMay's B-29s (the persistent enemy residents of Tokyo feared above all others) delivered a token farewell gift of many tons of *shoi-dan* (fire bombs) as well as five million leaflets warning the Japanese to surrender or suffer "utter destruction."

As if what had been served up so far was child's play.

That same night Lt. Col. Masataka Ida, who had just abandoned the idea of participating in a palace coup in Tokyo, had what he considered a smashing idea: he would lead the entire Japanese officer corps in mass suicide. He figured that would really get the attention of the foreign barbarians. The next day he and several adherents to this grandiose project conducted a straw poll among the few hundred officers available for questioning thereabouts, learning to their bitter disappointment that fewer than twenty percent of them would consider hara-kiri.

The night of August 14 was a busy one. The Emperor had recorded his surrender speech and a chamberlain concealed the record in a basement closet while participants in the palace coup dashed about trying to find and destroy it.

On August 15 the recording was broadcast to a shocked nation, none of whom had ever before heard the *Tsuru no koe* (Voice of the stork, i.e., the Emperor's voice).

Unnoticed (and even today little known) amid all this commotion Japan test-fired its own atomic weapon. The date was August 11, 1945.

The morning was cool in Konan, Korea. (Konan was the Japanese name for the place called Hungnam by the Koreans. It was the site of a gargantuan industrial complex, the largest in Korea under Japanese control.) A remote-controlled launch departed the tight security of the Konan docks, was guided a short distance across the choppy Sea of Japan, and entered the harbor of a small island.

For several days derelict boats and other aged vessels had been towed to the islet, so small it was not shown on most maps. The handful of resident fishermen had been sternly evacuated. When the robot launch came to a stop amid the derelict craft, its only passenger—an explosive atomic weapon—could not disembark unaided.

Twenty miles away, the observers waited with mounting anticipation. Wearing welder's goggles, they prayed that their years of assiduous effort would produce the awesome destruction the Japanese navy meant to unleash on the American invasion forces that autumn.

There it was! A ferocious ball of fire at least 1,000 yards in diameter. Vapors of many colors roiled toward the sky, eventually forming the same mushroom shape that overshadowed Hiroshima and Nagasaki.

Under the looming radioactive cloud the vessels in the small harbor had all either been sunk or were afire. All the vegetation on surrounding hillsides had been consumed leaving only smoking ashes.

When they well understood the effects of the tremendous force they had let loose, the Japanese scientists from the secret laboratory in Konan congratulated one another, immediately dispatching a message to what was left of their home office: the Rikken Laboratories outside Tokyo.

But their congratulations were moot. It was too late. This handful of gleeful atomic scientists would be among the last to know that Emperor Hirohito had already decided to surrender, sparing his nation any more death and devastation. The surrender terms were still being negotiated with the Allied Powers, but it was a "done deal." With heads bowed and eyes brimming, members of the Cabinet and Imperial High Command had heard the Emperor state, "I have decided to bring the war to an end." That meeting in the air-raid shelter under the Emperor's library had adjourned at 2:20, the morning of August 10, 1945.

Once news of the capitulation became known, the scientists in Konan across the Sea of Japan hastened to destroy all their records and as much of their equipment (including other nearly completed atom bombs) as possible, because Soviet trucks were already raising dust along the mountainous roads of northern Korea, heading south toward the Konan complex, which incidentally also comprised the largest fertilizer plant then in existence. Along with much else.

All equipment not destroyed by the Japanese was carted off to Russia. So were the Japanese nuclear scientists—to be tortured, interrogated, and erased from the pages of history.

What was the source of the information about the test? One Japanese officer who was entrusted with security at the research lab in Konan, who was interviewed shortly after the war by an American named David Snell, an agent with the 24th Criminal Investigation Detachment in Korea. After his army discharge Snell wrote an account of the interrogation that was published in the *Atlanta Constitution* in the summer of 1946.

David Snell's name can be found in *Who's Who in the South and Southwest*. He has been a *Life* magazine correspondent in Africa, Europe, and the Middle East, president of International Writers Ltd., and the winner of many journalistic awards, among them the prestigious George Polk Memorial. Snell is regarded as a reporter of unquestioned integrity.

Because the Russians had snapped their own locks on the gates of the Konan industrial complex, there was no way other correspondents could poke about to verify Snell's story or investigate it in greater depth. Most records in Japan had gone up in flames during B-29 raids or had been incinerated (or concealed) by the Japanese.

On November 23, 1945, American troops, having searched several partially destroyed laboratories, found five costly cyclotrons (devices central to the production of atomic bombs). These were forthwith dumped in the Pacific.

While Japanese and American scientists and researchers were outraged by such a senseless act of vandalism, not one person, unit, or agency could ever be found that acknowledged the responsibility for ordering it.

Japanese scientists had been studying the possibility of nuclear energy as far back as the twenties, but the effort to produce atomic bombs got its initial impetus after the formation of a committee of eleven of Japan's most prominent nuclear physicists and electronics scientists. They worked under a shroud of extreme secrecy, but it is known that the committee held its first meeting in Tokyo's Suikosha (Navy Club) on December 17, 1941. They were quickly confronted with a myriad of problems, among them locating a supply of uranium ore and deciding whether to seek and accept funding from the army or from the navy. Assignments of responsibility were made. University laboratories and commercial research organizations were designated for enlistment in the cause.

One of the committee members later admitted it was a shaky start, but at least they were all aboard and the vessel was getting up steam. The Japanese navy had already sponsored its own atomic weapons research with three of the eleven-member committee. Almost four years later the bomb tested off the coast of Konan, Korea, in August was built with Imperial Navy funds.

By then the Japanese knew the Americans (and British) would storm ashore in two places: Kyushu in November 1945 (landings on outlying islands would be made in late October) and on the beaches near Tokyo in the spring of 1946.

Operation Downfall was the code name assigned to both landings. Olympic would refer to the Kyushu effort and the beaches outside Tokyo would go by the name Operation Coronet.

The first landing—Olympic—would be a larger undertaking than Normandy. The entire Operation Downfall called for the services of the whole Marine Corps and every ship in the U.S. Pacific Navy.

Forty percent of all Americans then in uniform would take part. Logistically, Operation Downfall would be the most ambitious military or civilian project ever undertaken by the United States.

At his disposal General Douglas MacArthur would have one and a half million combat soldiers, with the support of three million more if needed, as well as eleven thousand aircraft and one hundred aircraft carriers backed by two hundred other Allied warships.

Dropping atom bombs into that mass of metal and flesh would have been like shooting fish in a barrel.

Ten American divisions would slated to land on Kyushu with four held in reserve on ships off-shore. Admiral William Leahy anticipated more than 150,000 American casualties in the campaign on Kyushu.

MacArthur's chief of intelligence, Gen. Charles Willoughby, who spoke with a Prussian accent but was very good at his job, estimated that four times that number of dead and wounded would constitute the "Butcher's bill" for the entire operation, should Downfall last until autumn 1946 (about half a year after the Coronet landings near Tokyo).

Section of a Japanese cyclotron, an integral mechanism used in constructing atomic bombs, being dumped in the sea near Yokohama by members of the US Army. *Courtesy of UPI/Corbis-Bettmann*

It was this almost certain concentration of America's military might that the Japanese navy had its sights set on as it frenetically urged more and more speed in the construction of as many as possible atom bombs like the one to be tested off Konan in August 1945.

Delaying construction of the atomic weapons were the swarms of silvery deadly B-29s that had brought the reality of war to Japan from late 1944 until the end of hostilities. Their raids had forced removal of the laboratories and construction machinery from several locations within Japan proper to the industrial complex at Konan, which was more secret but farther away. Three months were lost because of the need to dismantle and rebuild the production facility in Korea.

Japan's atom bombs would have been coming off the line in quantity by November 1945. Within a few hours they could have been loaded on any of the thousands of kamikaze aircraft hidden on air fields on Kyushu, and immediately off-shore: the bulk of the U.S. Pacific Fleet and hundreds of transport vessels carrying fourteen Americans and Allied divisions.

Of course, by then the Emperor had already sanctioned the surrender, but most of the top Japanese admirals and generals were stubbornly opposed to giving up. They came within an ace of having their way.

What is strange to contemplate in this scenario is the anathema that would presumably have clung to the Japanese if they had succeeded in dropping their own atomic bombs. Americans have been loudly abused for dropping "Little Boy" and "Fat Man." Would not the same opprobrium rain down as impartially on the heads of the Japanese if they had devastated the invasion fleet with similar weapons?

Writing in *Science*, a former U.S. ambassador to Japan (Edwin O. Reischauer) said, "I have always assumed that the Japanese would have done whatever they could to develop the atomic bomb during the war, and if they had it, would have used it."

Merely possessing nuclear bombs, buttressed by the commitment to use them as soon and as often as possible, surely qualifies the Japanese to share in any recriminations that only Americans have borne the brunt of until now.

### References

1. Wilcox, Robert K. *Japan's Secret War*. New York: Marlowe & Co., 1995.

2. *Pictorial History of the Second World War*, vol. 5. New York: Wm. H. Wise & Co., 1970.

3. Parrott, Lindsay. "Five Cyclotrons Wrecked in Japan." *New York Times*, November 24, 1945. (The *Times* reported further on the same topic on November 26 and 29 and on December 5, 6, 14, and 15, 1945).